INNER CITY MIRACLE

INNER CITY MIRACLE

JUDGE GREG MATHIS

WITH BLAIR S. WALKER

BALLANTINE BOOKS • NEW YORK

A Ballantine Book
Published by The Ballantine Publishing Group

Copyright © 2002 by Inner City Miracle, Inc.
Foreword copyright © 2002 by Reverend Jesse L. Jackson, Sr.

www.ballantinebooks.com

Library of Congress Cataloging-in-Publication Data can be
obtained from the publisher upon request.

ISBN 0-345-44642-9

Text design by Debbie Glasserman

Manufactured in the United States of America

First Edition: October 2002

10 9 8 7 6 5 4

I dedicate this book to my mother, Alice Lee Mathis,
who is responsible for all that I am;
to all the single mothers of the world;
and to all of America's troubled youth,
trying to overcome life's obstacles and challenges.

FOREWORD

Inner City Miracle chronicles Greg Mathis's journey from street youth to the youngest judge in Michigan history. The journey begins in the city of Detroit, Michigan, where Greg and his three brothers were raised by their single mother in the Herman Gardens housing projects.

Considered bright but incorrigible, Greg made poor choices and became a gang member who was expelled from four different schools and arrested several times. On his final encounter with the law, he received a visit, while in jail, from his ailing mother, who told him she was dying of cancer. Greg promised her that he would turn his life around, and so he began to persevere, rising beyond his circumstances.

Following his release from jail, Greg was ordered by a judge to earn a General Equivalency Diploma (G.E.D.). A year later, Greg entered college and, inspired by various civil rights and political activists—including Detroit mayor Coleman Young and myself—joined the movement for justice in America.

Greg earned his law degree and passed the Michigan bar examination. Despite challenges to his practicing law, due to his criminal record, Greg rose beyond the limitation of his environment, to become the youngest judge in Michigan history, and a nationally renowned television judge. I am proud to have contributed to Judge Mathis's commitment to fairness, justice, and push for excellence.

Inner City Miracle provides inspiration and direction for troubled youth, a model for parental expectations, and a moving testament to the value of lifting up America's youth, rather than locking them up.

—REVEREND JESSE L. JACKSON, SR.

ACKNOWLEDGMENTS

This book, or my life journey, would not have been possible without the love and assistance from God, my family, friends, and business associates. I thank God for my mother, Alice Lee Mathis, a single mother of four who instilled in me the spiritual and educational foundation that is most responsible for my success; my wife, Linda, and my children Amir, Gregory, Camara, and Jade, who have been and continue to be my foundation, my source of strength, and my pride and joy; my brothers Kenny, Steve, and Ron, who spoiled me and obeyed Mom's final request to stick together and go to church; my aunt Ethel, who helped raise me, and aunts Mitti, Edith, Gladys, and Eva, as well as my cousins, who've always supported me; my nieces and nephews who make me proud; my mother- and father-in-law Sylvia and Joe, who trusted me with their daughter and supported me when no one else would have; my mentors Addison Hines, Annette Rainwater, Councilman Cleveland and Reverend Jackson, who guided and helped me develop from street youth to judge; my best and lifelong friends, who support me and keep me grounded; Pastor Sheard and my church family, who keep me spiritually connected; my first production team, Ron, Theresa, and Earline, who helped convince the world we had a story to tell; George and Akbar, who helped present my story to Hollywood; Alonzo, Vic, Gus, and Walter, who presented my story to Warner Bros; the Brokaws and Mel, who presented my story to Ballantine Books; Anita and Blair, who crafted my story; Dick, Jim, and the other Warner Bros/Telepictures staff, who bring my show to television every weekday; and all my viewers who tune in.

PROLOGUE

Dangling from a cold metal railing on the second level of Cobo Hall Auditorium in downtown Detroit, I gaze down on thousands of unsuspecting concertgoers who actually think that a performance by the Average White Band is going to be the night's main event.

I say to myself, "It ain't about no damn band, you fools! If you don't believe it, check this shit out." Grinning, I plummet to the concrete nine feet below, which is fairly difficult to accomplish wearing platform shoes with four-inch clear plastic heels.

The impact sends a jolt crunching through my thin body and I stumble forward a few steps. I'd nearly dropped on the head of a young black male usher who is now frantically sprinting toward an exit. He's probably trying to alert the police, but it's a little late for that. The boldest mass robbery in Detroit's history is under way, and ain't nothin' he or anyone else can do to stop it!

The Errol Flynn gang is in the house and everybody at this concert had better give up some jewelry or a wallet. Either that or get cracked upside the head.

The year is 1977 and I'm in my element—lawlessness, chaos, and bold action.

The same holds true for two hundred or so of my fellow Errol Flynn gang members presently terrorizing the Cobo Hall Auditorium all around me during a brief intermission between musical acts. Some have actually vaulted onto the main stage while frightened and bewildered concertgoers look on.

"Errol Flynn, Errol Flynn!" I gleefully holler at the top of my lungs, matching the cadence of a handful of my homeboys who've commandeered the microphone onstage and are rhythmically waving their hands as they perform a popular 1970s dance called the Errol Flynn.

Like our movie star namesake, we Flynns fancy ourselves to be suave, swashbuckling, and rakish. And like the matinee idol whose name we carry, if we're trying to bust a move and you get in our way, we'll go upside your damn head.

Scanning a row full of Average White Band fans to my left, I see what I've really come to Cobo Hall for. As I look down the row, everyone on it is scowling mightily and shooting me expressions that leave no doubt about their fear and disgust. They have no way of knowing it, but the looks on their faces only heighten my tremendous sense of exhilaration.

I lock eyes with a young, muscular brother who has his hands protectively interlocked around his girlfriend's. His demeanor is defiant, as though he's feeling his oats and primed to do something heroic and macho.

I instinctually understand that if I break him down and force him to bend to my will, the entire row will meekly follow his lead.

"Your wallet, please," I bellow, giving my victim the hardest, meanest look I can muster. He shoots me a hard look right back, releases his girlfriend's hands and turns in my direction, preparing for battle. I expected that and slowly pull back the black pinstriped jacket of my double-breasted suit so he can see my ace in the hole—a .38-caliber revolver tucked in my waist.

Then with my eyes I silently dare him to continue his foolhardy challenge. Some concertgoers have already been punched and kicked for resisting, but things can get much, much worse. Reluctantly ceding defeat, my muscular victim sullenly digs into his back pocket, pulls out a brown leather wallet, and angrily flips it into the concrete aisle near my feet.

As I quickly bend over to retrieve my booty, the air inside Cobo Hall is filled with the noise of frantically chattering voices, the amplified racket from my partners onstage and screams of fear and pain. The sounds of bedlam and anarchy, sweet music to my ears.

"Thank you, sir. Gimme that watch, too."

The still-warm, expensive-looking silver timepiece is obediently passed down the row. Once the tough guy has been broken, my other victims quietly turn over their wallets, pocketbooks, bracelets, and rings, glaring at me the entire time. Like I could give a damn.

I barely have time to shake down half of another row before I need to make a hurried escape. Running as quickly as I can in my four-inch heels, I become part of a mass exodus of youthful thugs wearing platform-heeled shoes, double-breasted suits, Borsalino hats, wide-framed white glasses with no lenses.

Many of us are also toting expensive-looking umbrellas and walking canes, which come in handy when looking dapper or when scything through hordes of frenzied concertgoers.

As soon as I get outside Cobo Hall with the other Errol Flynns I spy black-suited, helmeted riot police standing shoulder-to-shoulder as they anxiously scan the exiting throng for lawbreakers.

They look stupid standing in the middle of the street with the streetlights glinting off their dark helmets. What do they expect me to do—walk up to them and surrender? Slowing down so that I'm moving at the same pace as the escaping concertgoers, I place a look on my face of consternation and fear that matches theirs. A wolf flowing to freedom among the panicked sheep. I gradually ease my way past the cops, who are nervously tapping their gloved hands with thick black billyclubs, looking for heads to lay siege to.

Battling a towering urge to run, I walk briskly down the sidewalk, each step taking me a little farther away from the scene of our crime. My crime!

But it's not until all the commotion and noise around Cobo Hall fade into the distance that I slow into a swaggering pimp walk, the stolen rings and watches in my jacket pockets jingling melodiously. The warm night air feels fantastic, thanks to a slight breeze fanning in off the Detroit River.

Only after I've walked a few yards does it dawn on me that I'm breathing pretty hard, not so much from exertion as from excitement. Even though the palms of my hands are moist and my stomach feels like a freight train is rumbling through it, I feel ecstatic.

A few blocks ahead a sea of dark Borsolino fedoras is bobbing down the street and I jog to catch up.

The cops were so worried about the safety of the concertgoers that they've left the rest of downtown unguarded, leaving the door open for a frenzied Errol Flynn gang looting spree. Soon store alarms are going off like crazy, punctuated by the brittle sound of storefront windows disintegrating. In no time the sidewalk is littered with glass shards that twinkle like diamonds under the streetlights and crunch underfoot.

Smiling, I saunter into Cousins, one of the premier clothing stores in downtown Detroit, and head straight for a hat rack at the far end of the darkened store. The store is filled with the fantastic odor of leather that emanates from expensive jackets and shoes neatly lined up on display. It's a smell I've always equated with wealth.

The leather looks tantalizing and I shoot an admiring glance as I hurriedly pass, headed toward my primary targets.

I have them in view now—two authentic Borsalino Como felt fur fedoras, painstakingly handcrafted in Alessandra, Italy. Taking off my fake fur Borsalino knockoff, I fling it into a corner, then slip the genuine article onto my Jeri-curled head. As soon as the baby-soft felt fur caresses my shoulder-length locks, I immediately understand why Comos are priced at $100 apiece.

Not to mention why they're the favored headgear of the top Detroit pimps and hustlers that I look up to.

With one Borsalino on my head and another in my hand, I bolt
out of Cousins and back onto the street, before the pigs start responding to all the jangling store alarms.

Feeling like a kid on Christmas morning, I eagerly make my way
back to the 1968 Camaro that my five-man crew and I parked several
blocks from Cobo Hall. I can't wait to divvy up the booty we've lifted
from the Average White Band crowd and I'm looking forward to seeing how the eleven o'clock news covers our audacious heist.

My boys and I have just ripped off several thousand Detroit concertgoers inside a major auditorium located mere blocks from police
headquarters.

1

BUTTERSCOTCH CANDY

Some folks love to slap a rags-to-riches tag on me, as though that somehow explains who I am and what I'm about.

But actually, my upbringing had nothing to do with rags or with gut-bucket poverty. I grew up in a highly regimented, strict household anchored by a no-nonsense mother who worked several jobs so that my three brothers and I would never go hungry or raggedy. We never went wanting for any of life's necessities, including discipline and love.

The first half of my life had to do with, as the old folks so quaintly put it, a hard head making for a soft ass. That is, until I finally figured out there was some merit to what Mama kept screaming and muttering and preaching while she was lighting up my tail with broom handles and whatever else she could wrap her strong hands around.

The child who put more gray in Alice Mathis's hair than any other was born in Detroit, Michigan, on April 5, 1960. I was a normal, healthy baby when I arrived on the scene in the maternity ward of Providence Hospital. But it wouldn't be long before I had Mama wondering if the last of her four boys was the devil's seed. I was by far the most defiant and incorrigible of my mother's offspring.

I say that with neither pride nor embarrassment. That's just how it was. Naturally I'll always regret the turmoil and pain Mama had to endure because of me, but I can never undo it.

All my acting out may have been a matter of the apple not falling far from the tree, because I'm told Mama was something of a hellion herself when she was a country girl growing up near Tallahassee, Florida. That's where my three brothers were born while my mother was married to her first husband.

Ronald, who is ten years older than me, came first, followed by Stephen two years later and then Kenneth, who's got six years on me. I'm not sure what happened to Mama's first marriage down in Florida, but I do know that at some point in the mid-1950s she packed up her brood and moved to Detroit. Raising three small boys by yourself in a strange city is nothing to be sneezed at, so you can appreciate where my independence, fire, and sense of self come from.

My mother did have a Detroit support mechanism in the person of my aunt Ethel, who worked as a physical therapist. Mama rented a small two-story house on Prairie Street and got a job as a waitress in a restaurant on the city's West Side.

One day while she was working, a charismatic young brother named Charles Mathis strolled into the eatery and sat down at one of Mama's tables.

The two of them struck up a conversation that blossomed into friendship and romance, culminating with a trip down the aisle and a new father figure for my three brothers. Personally, I have no recollection of growing up with my dad, because he split when I was about one year old.

I have no clue why he left his young family behind and, frankly, I've never cared to hash over the details. Mom was always there for me and that's all I ever needed to know.

So I started life on Prairie Street surrounded by three quasi–father figures named Ron, Steve, and Ken. We grew up in a black working-class neighborhood on the West Side that was surrounded by noisy auto factories, which filled the air with the sound of clattering machinery and the smells of oil and chemicals. One facility, a foundry owned by Ford, had an area with spectacular flames always billowing out.

Prairie Street was filled with hardworking families where the father typically drew a paycheck from a factory owned by Ford, General Motors, Chrysler, or American Motors, while the mother stayed at home and rode herd on children, housework, and meals.

The modest two-story houses on Prairie Street had only three feet of separation between them and were made of wood. They may as well have been row houses, because you could hear everything that your neighbors were doing anyway.

Big flakes of peeling paint mushroomed from most of the houses on my block, but a few households took pains to keep their dwellings freshly painted and neat-looking at all times.

There was plenty of asphalt and concrete in my neighborhood but only a handful of small trees. Quite a few moms cultivated tidy flower or vegetable gardens in the rear on the little postage-stamp parcels of land that passed for backyards.

From a socioeconomic standpoint, Prairie Street was made up of an interesting mix of folks who were lower-middle-class and poor. It may not have been the most affluent neighborhood in Detroit, but our street was kept free of trash and dust. On summer afternoons the mothers on my block would drag their kids outside, and then everyone would sweep the sidewalks, as well as the front steps of homes.

Like the other houses on the block, mine had three small bedrooms and a basement that remained nice and cool even during the dog days of summer. Ken and I shared one bedroom, Ron and Steve had another, and Mama had one to herself. We did not live in squalor, because Mama continually made sure that her sons tidied up around the house and kept it spotless. The smell of Mr. Clean was always hanging in the air, along with Pine-Sol and Clorox, Mama's favorite cleaning agents.

But I loved it best when our home on Prairie Street reeked of collard greens bubbling on the stove. That meant that in a little while I'd be chowing down on fried chicken, candied yams, and collard greens, my favorite meal to this day. Mama could burn when it came to whipping together a pot roast or baked salmon, too.

Following dinner, we would put our dishes into the kitchen sink and Mama or one of my older brothers would wash them. Once the table had been cleared, Mama would dig out a medium-sized Bible with a greenish brown cover. Its pages were frayed and sullied from constant use. The entire family would sit around our wooden kitchen table and Mama would lead us in a devotion session.

In her strong, soothing voice she read passages from the Bible, then discussed them or asked one of her sons for an interpretation. Our discussion would be followed by a family prayer, my signal that it was about time for me to hit the sack.

Kids who got in trouble on Prairie Street ran the risk of having their behinds smoked by someone else's mother, who would then notify your parents after she was finished—guaranteeing that you'd receive another fierce whipping once you got home. There was a sense of caring and sharing on Prairie Street that I have never experienced since.

When I was small, I thought that the world was black, because my environment on Prairie Street was all African American. The only time I saw significant numbers of white people was on June 30—the day Detroit displays its July 4th fireworks. On that date hundreds of thousands of Detroiters gather on the banks of the Detroit River to watch as a brilliant fireworks display explodes across the night sky.

On June 30 I would see whites and blacks happily mingling as the delicious smell of grilling hamburgers and hotdogs wafted through hordes of relaxed people milling about shoulder-to-shoulder. One of my brothers usually had a firecracker or a stink bomb that they'd let me set off when Mama wasn't looking.

Once the fireworks display ended, Mama would herd us back to our car and we'd return to our all-black world.

There was a corner near my Prairie Street house where, in the summertime when the sun began to set, a group of four or five brothers would congregate like clockwork to warble a cappella doo-wop ditties as they passed around a wine bottle wrapped in a brown paper bag.

Initially there wasn't much of a criminal element around except for the unkempt, incoherent heroin junkies who sometimes wobbled along through the alley behind my house, their glazed eyes fixed on nothing in particular. Aside from getting high all the time, the other thing they excelled at was leaving a trademark dried-urine smell everywhere they went.

Practically everyone detested the junkies and looked down their noses at them, but I found them fascinating just because they ignored all of Prairie Street's unwritten rules, including the ones saying that you slaved from nine to five every day, moaned constantly about bills, and spent Sundays sitting in a boring-ass church for hours on end. They didn't give a shit what society said or thought about their drug-addled lifestyle. So I didn't see the junkies as pitiful people bumbling around in a narcotic stupor—I saw them as independent souls to be admired.

While I may have thought they were cool, I never wanted to be one of them. Because it was apparent their worldly possessions were usually the dirty clothes on their backs.

My earliest career aspiration was to become a firefighter. That may have lasted a year or two before it was replaced by a burning desire to become a pimp and a hustler. Why? Because their pockets were always full of money, they were often accompanied by foxy women, and they drove really slick, expensive American luxury cars.

When one of them would glide down Prairie Street behind the wheel of a Cadillac, me and the other young dudes would crane our necks and check out his every move. We would go, "Wow! I wonder what his hustle is? And look at that bad shit he got!" We'd take in the expensive threads, flashy pinky rings, industrial-strength cologne, and stylish full-length fur coats and dream of one day acquiring the same kinds of things for ourselves.

The husbands and fathers of Prairie Street provided a jarring contrast that I never aspired to: They'd trudge home after a grueling day's work in some dirty factory, lugging a lunch pail, looking tired and beat down and smelling like machine oil.

Me and the other boys on Prairie Street received an unspoken lesson from watching all this: If you don't want to have much in the way of money or opportunity as a black man, become a part of the mainstream.

We also noticed that the well-behaved, studious kids on the block never had any money. It followed, then, that there was no sense in sitting in a classroom all day, because we'd never met anybody who'd made money doing that.

So my whole mind-set early in life was to go against the grain. I was defiant against society and everything that it stood for. My having no use for structure, framework, or rules put me on an obvious collision course with my mother, because Lord knows Mama had enough rules for six or seven households.

"Do your homework as soon as you get home!"

"We're going to church every Friday, Saturday, and Sunday, do you hear me?"

"Don't you boys go see any movies—that garbage is the devil's work!"

Mama was a Seventh-Day Adventist who took her religion *seriously.* I was fifteen before I ever set foot in a movie theater, and I had to sneak in when I finally did. That's because our religion had decreed motion pictures the work of the devil.

Seventh-Day Adventists follow many of the same prohibitions and rules observed by Jews, meaning that I never tasted shellfish as a child and never got to eat catfish either, which is viewed as being an unclean fish because of its scavenger eating habits.

From sundown Friday till sundown Saturday, my brothers and I literally weren't allowed to do anything, not even watch TV, because of Mama's beliefs. When I hear the sons and daughters of Baptist and Methodist Holy Rollers complaining about their strict upbringing, I just smile. Because none of their stories come close to approaching what I had to go through.

For one thing, I couldn't wear a school ring around my mother.

Why? Because the Seventh-Day Adventists banned the wearing of jewelry.

A tall, dark-skinned, heavyset woman with high cheekbones, Mama would have looked great in lipstick, but her religion decreed that women couldn't wear makeup of any kind. Fortunately, my mother's regal face and skin were beautiful without it.

Our house was a sanctified bastion of spirituality, but just outside its walls lurked wild West Detroit in all its sinful, secular glory. In my early years I bounced back and forth between those incredibly different worlds, barely tolerating one and lusting for the other with all my heart.

I knew that what my mother wanted for me was probably best, but the Seventh-Day Adventist Church was much too restrictive and confining for my wild ass.

Mama was well aware of this and viewed herself as fighting a holy war for the hearts and minds of her impressionable boys—not to mention the salvation of our immortal souls. It was a losing battle where I was concerned, because the dry, humorless Seventh-Day Adventists couldn't hold a candle to the thrills and chills to be found in the streets on a daily basis.

So I led a double life growing up and tended to view myself as different because of that. I felt like a big punk around my boys because I am somewhat light-skinned, was going to church three times a week, couldn't see movies, and so on. I hoped my posse didn't notice my differences, but they easily saw what time it was. They used to bombard me with insults and challenges.

"Why you always in church if you so slick, *Church Boy?*"

It killed me so much to be thought of as a Holy Roller, a goody two-shoes, that I overcompensated. When I started walking the wrong path, I swaggered down that bad boy with a vengeance. It was all an effort on my part to avoid being perceived as soft—getting my props has always been a huge thing with me.

And one thing I craved was respect from my older brothers. So I acted out around the house to show them I was as tough as they were. This put me in conflict with Mama, who would take a belt or an extension cord to my bare butt whenever she reached her limit with my foolishness.

While my backside was still throbbing, I cried and screamed and promised God to change my wicked ways. And I would hold true to that . . . for a day or two. Then the welts on my behind would disappear and I'd fall back into the same hardheaded routine that landed me in trouble in the first place.

Along with the respect thing, something else that I've dealt with my entire life is a short attention span. To be honest, I probably had a mild case of attention deficit disorder as a child. So I gravitated toward things that snagged my attention big time, that got my adrenaline flowing and my heart pumping hard, as opposed to things that called for me to sit and be inactive. Like those loooooong worship session in our Seventh-Day Adventist church.

I was a typical energetic African American boy who needed the no-nonsense guidance of a strong man committed to being a good father. Since I didn't have that growing up, the main male role models I patterned myself after were my peers. Unfortunately, most of them were on an express track to nowhere.

My mother had a very close friend on Prairie Street named Mattie Fears, who had six girls and three boys. One of them, an ol' lanky waterhead boy named Alonzo Fears, was my ace and one of my main partners in crime.

"Sputnik," as we called Alonzo, would break my heart later in life by fatally overdosing after taking a speedball, a scary combination of heroin and cocaine.

One day when we were small boys, our mothers dragged Sputnik and me to Atlantic Spartans, a sprawling department store that used to be very popular in Detroit. Our moms took us there to buy us new shoes, but once that mission was accomplished they did a little browsing, as womenfolk tend to do. Naturally this bored Sputnik and me to tears.

Seeing that our mothers weren't really paying us any attention, and looking for an excitement fix, Sputnik and I broke away and went on a little shoplifting spree.

Basically, Sputnik and I had been emulating the older boys on Prairie Street, who would go into stores and boost cartons of cigarettes, then return to our block and find plenty of eager buyers for their stolen wares. Stealing was a big deal and all the older guys were doing it.

So when Sputnik and I were in Atlantic Spartans bored to death, broke, and feeling our candy jones coming down, we asked ourselves how the other boys in the neighborhood got what they wanted. The answer, of course, was they stole it! We simply followed the behavioral model that had been laid out for us.

We couldn't have been more than five years old and our skills weren't terribly refined. If you're going to shoplift candy, it doesn't make much sense to eat it before you even get it out of the store. But that made perfect sense to the two of us, so it only took a few minutes for us to get pinched by Atlantic Spartans security guards.

Tears were streaming down my face and snot was flying out of my nose when one of those white men snatched me and dragged me back to Mama, my pockets brimming with pilfered butterscotch candy. I was crying because I was genuinely afraid of my mother's reaction once she found out what I had done.

As expected, she set off an atomic bomb on my backside after that episode. The ass-whipping she laid on me definitely got my attention, but it wasn't enough to make me quit shoplifting cold turkey.

Stealing department store candy may seem innocent or funny, but there's nothing cute about it. Practically every career criminal cuts his or her teeth on petty crimes like shoplifting. It's a rare person who begins as a stickup artist or a cat burglar. Like any other profession, you have to work your way to the top.

BAD BOY, MAMA'S BOY

Mama was determined to keep all four of her boys on the straight and narrow. Especially her youngest. With that in mind, she moved us from Prairie Street into a Detroit public housing project that was 80 percent white when we arrived there in 1965. Poor whites engage in just as much criminal activity as poor blacks do, so I guess Mama's main objective was to get me away from my little thug friends on Prairie Street.

The Herman Gardens housing project was alien territory. It had mostly white tenants and massive expanses of green grass, pretty, fragrant flowers, and neatly trimmed shrubbery. In time the project's racial complexion would change dramatically due to white flight—the place was totally black within five years of my moving there.

Like most public housing projects of that time, I believe Herman Gardens was built in the 1950s for GIs who had served in World War II. In the 1960s you needed to have a connection with someone in city government to get in, like Diana Ross and her family did when they lived in Detroit's Brewster projects.

I'm not sure who Mama called a chit with to get her brood into Herman Gardens, but she pulled it off.

Herman Gardens marked my first encounter with racism. Before that, it was just an abstraction that I'd heard older blacks talk about.

It was a fairly common occurrence at Herman Gardens for young black and white people to wage racially motivated skirmishes, because we were right on a dividing line between a black and a white community. At nearby Cody High School, black students were outnumbered, so black kids from other schools would come to help fight white kids.

Around the time we moved into Herman Gardens, they used to open up Cody High to the community for evening recreation sessions. My little buddies and I were on our way to one of those sessions one evening when we ran into members of a white motorcycle gang. We sensed they were up to no good and scampered for our lives as members of the gang pursued us and threw chains at us. That was a terrifying experience I honestly wasn't sure I was going to live to tell about.

Once I started experiencing racism firsthand and saw there was a problem between black and white people, all white people became suspect to me. It wasn't that I hated all white people or anything, because I had a handful of white friends at Herman Gardens. But if you were white and I didn't know you, I just automatically assumed that you were prejudiced until your actions proved otherwise. Unfortunately, most of the time that assumption proved right on the money.

As a little boy I watched white police officers routinely hassle and search black folks for absolutely no reason other than skin color, and I recall how the white kids wouldn't let black kids play on Herman Gardens's asphalt basketball court.

Something else I remember vividly is my friends and me being called "nigger" by white kids. The first time I heard that ugly word directed in my direction, I punched the hateful mouth that uttered it. I never said a word to my mother about that little altercation.

My oldest brother, Ronald, admired the Black Panthers, and he said it was high time for black folks to stop taking abuse from whites.

So I heeded his advice and made it a point not to take any guff from white kids.

My friends and I took things a step further and put a Robin Hood twist on matters. Every time we got a chance, we took from the rich and gave to the poor by jacking up any white boy unlucky—or stupid—enough to be by himself when we happened to be around Herman Gardens.

We saw white boys as weaker, and we jumped on them and took their money and possessions regularly. On the other hand, if you let a white boy take your shit, you were viewed as weak, as somebody who was "lame." Looking back I realize that my anger against whites was misplaced.

But when I was at Herman Gardens, I would rather have died than be seen as lame. To prove my toughness, I thrust myself into a lot of dumb situations where an itchy trigger finger could easily have taken me out.

I was a complex mix of styles and motivations. I was a church boy, a bad boy, and, truth be told, a mama's boy.

Check this out—another area in which I lived a double life was academics. I may have been a hoodlum and a troublemaker, but I always got As and Bs in school.

Mama initially enrolled me in Herman Gardens Elementary School. As far as I was concerned, elementary school was just another venue where I could challenge authority and give adults a run for their money.

I used to regularly pull pranks like putting tacks on my teacher's chair when she wasn't looking. And if she was careless enough to turn her back to the class, she could count on a Greg Mathis spitball smacking her upside the head.

My first teacher was Mrs. McGivens, a white woman who weighed three hundred pounds if she weighed one. I was one of her prime disciplinary problems, and I have no doubt that Mrs. McGivens hated my little black ass. I did something one day that finally caused Mrs. McGivens to lose it, because she reached down and smacked me in the face! She hit me so hard that the outline of her hand remained on my face. I've already told you that she was a hefty woman, so you can imagine what her hand felt like when it came crashing down on my pointy little head. I saw stars afterward and was still crying uncontrollably as I walked home, still stunned by the force of Mrs. McGivens's blow.

When I walked through the front door and Mama got an eyeful of Mrs. McGivens's handprint, she immediately jumped up from her chair at the kitchen table and starting scowling and muttering. She wasted no time tracking down her thick black leather belt. That legal stuff about being innocent until proven guilty didn't apply in my household, not when I was the suspect.

"Whatever that teacher said you did, YOU PROBABLY DID!" Mama said in a low, scary voice that raised the hair on my neck. "So come on and let me whip you. But she was wrong for hitting you in your face. She should whip your *behind,* not your face."

Once Mama got finished beating the tar out of me, she made me dry my tears and wash my face. Then she hustled me out the door and we moved doubletime in the direction of Herman Gardens Elementary School. It seemed that in the minute or so it took us to get there, Mama actually got madder and more agitated than she had been when she walked out our front door.

Even though she was a strict Seventh-Day Adventist, I could hear her quietly cussing to herself. I slumped my shoulders as we walked into my school, figuring another whippin' was probably in the offing.

Mama already knew where Mrs. McGivens's room was. She didn't even stop at the principal's office—she marched straight to my first-grade classroom, which was decorated with pictures of cute yellow ducklings and baby bunny rabbits.

When Mrs. McGivens saw us coming, she immediately rose from her desk and started striding toward Mama. Pointing indignantly to the hand outline still on my face, my mother roared, "Did you do this to him?"

Just as Mrs. McGivens started to respond, I watched in absolute amazement as Mama's right hand streaked toward my first-grade teacher's face! *Patow!* Just like that, my mother had slapped one of Mrs. McGivens's fat pink cheeks hard as hell.

You know how sometimes your eyes see things that don't register on your brain right away? Seeing Mama slap the piss out of Mrs. McGivens was like that for me. It took a couple of stunned seconds before I fully comprehended what I had just seen.

As big as Mrs. McGivens was, she took two or three steps backward, Mama hit her so hard.

The next thing I knew, my mother's strong hand encircled mine and I was dragged out of Mrs. McGivens's classroom. "Come on, let's get out of here before I *really* hurt that woman!"

Not only did Mama's overhand right end her conversation with Mrs. McGivens, it also brought my educational career at Herman Gardens Elementary School to a close.

With her mission accomplished, Mama slowly walked back home, still steaming and muttering. I tagged along a half step behind, deathly afraid to utter a single word. Mama never said anything to me as we walked home, so I kept my eyes straight ahead and my mouth shut.

One thing I can tell you about Mama is that she took that eye-for-an-eye stuff in the Bible very seriously. I was probably scared straight for a good week after she fired on my teacher like that. And I'll bet anything that it was a long, long time before Mrs. McGivens put her beefy hands on another student again, if she ever did.

Rightfully feeling that Detroit's public schools had failed her and her youngest child, Mama enrolled me in the Peterson Seventh-Day Adventists Academy. Fortunately, I knew a lot of the students there, because I spent Fridays and Saturdays holed up in church with many of them. Most were bourgeois-acting, middle-class blacks, possibly because they had heard their mothers and fathers say that it cost something like $120 a month to attend Peterson.

How Mama scraped up that tuition every month I will never know, but she must have sacrificed big time to send me to Peterson. To put that $120 monthly tuition in perspective, Mama was only paying $80 every month for the three-bedroom project unit her entire family lived in.

When I arrived at Peterson, the scouting report on Greg Mathis went like this: "He's poor and he's bad, but he's smart." I went in there believing my advance billing and intent on fulfilling it. My self-identity had been formed by first grade—bad, but smart.

Every time the teacher asked a question, my grubby hand would be the first to shoot into the air. On the other hand, I was the most unruly person in the entire school. The principal and teachers at Peterson expected students to be smart *and* well-behaved. My refusal to get in line with those expectations resulted in me getting paddled once a week by the principal or a teacher, because Peterson was big on corporal punishment.

Most of the other kids attending Peterson were stuck up and never really accepted me, so I never bought into what they represented, either. They always looked down on me, so I always had this "fuck you" attitude toward them: "I'm still the man, I'm smarter than y'all, and if anybody doesn't like it, I'll beat your asses to boot!"

I've always had high self-esteem and a strong sense of self. I've always believed I could excel at whatever I wanted to, whether it was school or sports or hustling in the streets. That benefited me for the rest of my life, and so did moving to Herman Gardens. Living around white folks taught me that I could be just as good, if not better, than they were at anything.

So basically I felt like I had the measure of white kids, black kids—it really didn't matter to me. As for the well-to-do black kids at Peterson, I viewed them with utter contempt, because as far as I was concerned they were all punks and I was a tough street kid. I admired tough-guy types, not little nerds who obediently did everything they were told!

We didn't wear ties and uniforms at Peterson, but most of the students came there dressed in clothes that were dull, boring, and oh so conservative. I, on the other hand, was flashy as could be.

Of course none of the other students dared comment on my attire because even though I was a small, skinny kid, the word out on Greg Mathis was that he could fight and that he was crazy. So no one befriended me, really, other than the other poor kids. Out of a class of twenty, there were maybe two or three others who were from backgrounds similar to mine and who could identify with me.

Mr. Bradford, the principal, was a huge man who was about six-foot-five, had a big head on his massive shoulders, and was about my complexion. He spoke in this tremendous, booming voice that could be heard throughout the school.

An authoritarian individual, Mr. Bradford sometimes seemed to think that his primary job was to regularly spank my ass. I got whippings for talking all the time, for mumbling under my breath, for cursing other kids, and for taking their money.

I plead guilty to all of those charges.

Yet there was a side to me that had to show those bourgeois black kids that I could outperform them academically, too. I've always had a desire to be respected among my peers regardless of what environment I find myself in. So I was always a B-plus student at Peterson, even though I probably received more beatings than any other elementary student in the school's history.

That pattern continued until Peterson finally got fed up with me and kicked me out when I was in the fourth grade. So then Mama put me in a white Seventh-Day Adventist school in a white part of northwest Detroit. The school was about five miles from the Herman Gardens projects. I lasted there two years until they also kicked me out. By that time I was in the sixth grade.

Mama beat a tattoo on my ass while I was in elementary school, but I just wasn't going to do right. Clearly, my upbringing had nothing to do with sparing the rod and spoiling the child. The rod was used frequently, but I reveled in being a bad seed. It was as simple as that. No paddles, belts, or electric cords were going to change my mind. Greg Mathis was determined to choose the path he walked, not to leave that choice to teachers, principals, or parents.

My competitive, proud nature wouldn't allow me to be a half-ass thug or a half-ass student. In every realm in which I chose to participate, it was important for me to show people that I was as good as they were—or better.

I was fully aware that Mama was very, very unhappy with my inability to follow rules and conduct myself as if I had common sense. However, the folks I respected the most and spent the most time with were my brothers and my boys.

I had a clear choice—devote myself to pleasing Mama and get beaten up and ridiculed every damn day—or prove that I was tough enough to hang in an increasingly hostile environment, due to the tensions between blacks and whites in Herman Gardens.

Mama unwittingly helped decide which path I would take by making me share a bedroom with my brother Kenny in our three-bedroom Herman Gardens home.

Kenny was my bosom buddy, even though he's six years older. I emulated Kenny and his friends in every possible way, and I tried to stay within their orbit as much as I could. Kenny would try to keep me away, but Mama often forced Kenny to take me with him. Thanks to my natural inclinations and those pushes from Mama, I learned a lot of bad things from Kenny and his friends.

My mother wanted me to spend time with Kenny because she was away from home so much. She had two jobs during our Herman Gardens days. One was a nurse's aide position at Henry Ford Hospital, where she worked the night shift. During the day, Mama would drive her used white Ford Fairlane 500 to suburban Grosse Point, where she worked as a housekeeper. I really didn't see much of Mama because most of my time was consumed by school, and after I got home she would nap from six-thirty until ten to get ready for Henry Ford Hospital.

That left me and my brothers with lots of time when we weren't under her direct supervision.

While I was sharing a bedroom with Kenny and bugging him to death, my other brothers Steve and Ron were sharing a room, too.

Ron, who is ten years older than me, and Steve, who is eight years older, used to fight all the time. Steve was a happy-go-lucky guy, while Ron was very serious.

I learned a lot about militancy from Ron. That was the only part of his personality that attracted me to him, because everything else about him was too square for my tastes. But I liked the fact that he was involved in something that taught you how to fight white people. I somewhat looked up to Ron, but he was so serious all the damn time. He was mean and aloof, too.

I never saw that much of Steve, because he was absolutely in love with the streets and the party life. He definitely had a thing for the fast life.

One thing I remember about my two oldest brothers is that they were always getting put out of the house by Mama. She would take their keys when evicting them, too.

"Get out and don't come back, until you're ready to do what I tell you to do. I don't care where you stay—go where you were when you didn't come home on time last night."

The tough love Mama showed me and my brothers meant that once you were fifteen and too big to be whipped, you got thrown out for breaking her rules. You could only get back by begging and promising to act right.

It was usually Steve that Mama had to kick out, because Ron spent a lot of his time studying so he could do well in high school. I'm glad Ron was one kid Mama didn't have to worry about much, because she had to worry about me all the time. In a bid to keep me out of devilment, Mama typically ordered Kenny to supervise me, which made it possible for the two of us to get into devilment together, along with Kenny's best friend, Rick.

At first Kenny and I made an effort to stay inside while our mother slept. We would pass the time away with a card game, usually tonk or blackjack. The stakes always started at a quarter a game, but they didn't usually end there. Later I became proficient at rolling dice.

That skill came in handy, because winning allowed me to buy candy and eventually wine, cigarettes, and weed.

Not surprisingly, Kenny beat me at will when I first started playing, which was when I was around eight years old. Losing infuriated me to no end—sometimes I would cry tears of frustration to Kenny's delight.

But after a while, I got to the point where I started to beat Kenny. Whenever I did, he would glare at me and bark, "You little muthafucka!" That was always his response whenever I flashed my superior wit or intelligence.

But the last thing Kenny wanted to do was remain cooped up inside our place all the time with his little brother. At the age of fourteen, naturally, his hormones were raging. However, the price of freedom from our Herman Gardens apartment was having to drag me with him. So in time he began to come up to me and say, "Man, you wanna go somewhere with me and Rick?"

And I'd light up like a Christmas tree. Oh yeah.

I became very good at manipulating my brothers to get things I wanted, particularly when it came to Kenny. Whenever he and his crew tried to sneak off without me, my standard threat was: "Take me, or I'm tellin' Mama." It worked every time.

But Kenny was smart enough to know that I shouldn't be out after dark with him. If I was caught out with him, he would be in big trouble in terms of a whipping and other punishment.

That didn't pose much of a problem at first, because initially we only went outside to sit on a portico situated on the grounds of Herman Gardens. Made of wood and painted white, the portico was a place to find shelter from sudden summer showers, as well as a place where you could relax on some wooden benches and just chill. The structure was about one hundred feet from the unit where I lived and served as connector between our building and other buildings in the complex.

The portico was a meeting place where the young, bored black males of Herman Gardens used to gather to smoke weed, drink wine, and sing '60s songs. The most popular ditties were those sung by the immortal Temptations, and everybody fantasized about becoming the next great Motown act.

My mother didn't have a big problem with me going to the portico, even if I wasn't being supervised by one of my brothers.

Like many large cities, Detroit was roiled by urban unrest during the 1960s. Something that made quite an impression on my young brain was the Detroit riots of 1967. I vividly recall that a curfew had been established, and that National Guardsmen were riding around Herman Gardens brandishing pistols, rifles, and machine guns. As the Guardsmen flitted around looking for curfew breakers, army tanks rumbled up and down the main avenue near our housing complex! It's a good thing they never caught up with my brothers Ron and Steve, who were out looting.

The Detroit police department was oppressive in the '60s, but they really went buck wild after the '67 riots. There was a particularly brutal group of foot patrolmen nicknamed the Big Four who began showing up at Herman Gardens after the riots. These four notorious cops were in their thirties, burly, and always toting around shotguns. They would search and seize you every time they laid eyes on you. Even if you hadn't done anything wrong, that didn't keep you from getting thrown on the ground and searched, then driven to a police precinct where you were fingerprinted and placed in a lineup. So you might as well be doing something wrong when you encountered the Big Four.

Many years later when I was trying to get my law license, I was turned away because of my arrest record. The Michigan bar people were like, "Wow, look at this arrest record!" The sad truth is that I never committed many of the crimes that I was arrested for. Most people would have a pretty scary arrest record if the police were always carting them down to the police station for sport. Just about every young black male in Herman Gardens had a record like that.

Sometimes, the Big Four would send you home with a knot on your head, depending on how you acted and how you looked. If you were dressed a certain way or had a certain demeanor like, they would go off on you. The Big Four viewed t zookeepers, and young black males were the animals.

Future Detroit mayor Coleman Young was later elected ~~~ pledge to quell police brutality by getting more officers of color into the department.

Eventually things got so bad that it became great sport to sit on the roof of the portico and take potshots at the police with .22-caliber and .38-caliber pistols. The white folks had long since fled by that point.

Sometimes we would use zip guns, because it was hard to come by a handgun back in those days (you had to break into somebody's house to get one). After the shots had been fired, we'd haul ass for all we were worth because about fifty cops would be swarming all over Herman Gardens in a matter of minutes. Once the excitement had died down, we'd do it all over again. Fortunately, no policeman ever got shot.

But it's no exaggeration to say that everyone at Herman Gardens was scared shitless of the Big Four. Nobody dared to clamber up on the portico and take a potshot at them. It was generally agreed that if they even *thought* a round had been fired at them from the direction of the portico, they'd first light up the entire structure with their twelve-gauge shotguns, then ask questions.

Given the environment that I grew up in and the fact that I had fairly limited contact with my mother, it shouldn't come as a shock that I was a chronic thief by the time I was eight or nine.

Basically, no matter how hard she tried and how hard she prayed, Mama was destined to lose control over me. I spent six hours a day at school, where I had at least four hoodlum friends, and another four hours a day with the thugs in the projects while my mother was taking her nap. So who am I going to try and fit in with—Mama, who I'm spending three hours a day with at most, or the kids with whom I spend ten hours a day?

And remember that these same kids will whip my butt and take my clothes and my money if they feel I don't deserve their respect.

The whole time I was going places with Kenny and his best friend, Rick, I was also associating with street kids closer to my age. I would teach the guys in my age group little scams that Kenny had taught me, while they were teaching me tricks they'd picked up from their dads, uncles, and brothers.

Most of my escapades took place after bribing or threatening Kenny to let me out of the house. Once I had escaped the penitentiary known as my apartment, I would often ride my bicycle to Prairie Street, which was a couple of miles away from Herman Gardens. The other boys my age on Prairie Street were smoking weed and cigarettes openly, so I fell in with that, too. Not because I had any particular love for either, but because I didn't want to be viewed as a wimp who was too scared to be down with the fellas.

We reveled in our bad-boy aura, such as it was. A favorite tactic was to travel to a corner grocery store, flooding it about five or six strong. That would give the person behind the counter fits because they would figure out what we were up to as soon as we trooped in. Since it's impossible to keep track of six energetic little knuckleheads flitting all over the place simultaneously, it was an effective way to rob the place blind, then quickly leave.

The first time I ever took a drink was in the alley behind Prairie Street. Drinking was something of a rite of passage, because we no longer viewed ourselves as innocent babes once alcoholic spirits had entered our bodies. In our little eight-year-old minds, drinking alcohol made us worldly and sophisticated. The big boys did it, so we did, too.

Someone had sneaked a fifth of rum out of their parents' house, along with a paper cup. We didn't even have enough sense to dilute the rum with Coke or ice. When I put the golden liquid to my lips, it tasted nasty and burned my throat going down. I really wanted to spit it out, but I wasn't about to do that in front of my boys. Anyway, the two guys who drank in front of me hadn't spit out their rum, so I wasn't about to be the first.

That rum may have been nasty, but one thing I've never acquired a taste for is beer. To this day I still don't like it. Cigarettes, on the other hand, were no problem. I started smoking when I was about seven or eight. I used to follow old men around and wait until they tossed their cigarette butts, then pick them up and sniff on them.

Of course, I was learning deviant behavior back at the Herman Gardens projects, too. The white kids at Herman Gardens taught me how to sniff glue and lighter fluid. This was probably when I was around nine years old. I'd get together with some of the bad white kids, and we'd steal some glue from a store. We even had a little slogan: "Airplane glue, one sniff and whooooo!"

The white kids used to say that if you took a deep hit of glue and then listened closely, you could hear the sound of freight trains rumbling inside your head. I usually placed the glue on a sheet of toilet paper or squirted it inside a paper bag. Then I'd take a real deep breath to make sure the vapors went into my lungs. That would bring a feeling of euphoria for a couple of minutes, before it died down. Then I'd repeat the process.

I couldn't have my boys on Prairie Street remaining in the dark about this, so I turned them on to it, too.

But the whole time I was acting like a so-called tough guy, I was still sleeping in my mother's bed whenever I had an opportunity! She began trying to break me of that habit when I was about eight, but I had an answer for that.

During the two nights a week when she wasn't working, I'd crawl on the floor into her room, then get into bed with her and cuddle up.

Some big-time gangster, huh?

But make no mistake about it—when I was away from Mama and with my boys, I was a different person. I prided myself on being seen as the craziest, the most ruthless, and the most unpredictable of my crew.

After my family had been at Herman Gardens about two years, a couple of black boys my age who also belonged to my Seventh-Day Adventist Church moved into the housing project. David and Robert were fantastic cohorts.

Usually the three of us would hook up with three other black kids, and we would all troop to a Kmart store up the street from Herman Gardens. That Kmart came to be our favorite target for shoplifting.

Another frequent activity was stealing boxes of steaks from the grocery market, then selling them to the folks in the projects. If you were willing to break the law and were even remotely enterprising, there was plenty of money to be made.

My posse and I learned most of our Crime 101 lessons inside stores near Herman Gardens, before we graduated to snatching purses and boosting bicycles and minibikes. From there we progressed to a more advanced curriculum that included stealing cars and eventually armed robbery.

Criminality and getting high tend to go hand-in-hand. By the time I was ten I was swigging wine all the time. Mama was always away at one of her two jobs, so she never had an opportunity to sniff the alcohol on my breath.

Boone's Farm was the starter wine of choice among the fellas, because it was so sweet and contained so little alcohol that it wasn't much different from drinking Kool-Aid.

However, I definitely can't say that about the next wines on the menu, MD 20/20 and Richard's Wild Irish Rose. Mad Dog 20/20, as the first one was nicknamed, and Richard's were both cheap and contained so much alcohol that they packed a wallop like a mule's kick. Several of us could get buzzed from one bottle, but those wines would tap dance all over a youthful stomach if you weren't careful.

While everybody wanted to get high, nobody wanted to cross the line that caused you to retch your brains out in front of the boys. That wasn't cool, to say the least. Plus the poor victim could count on being the butt of jokes for days.

The main reason I did drugs, alcohol, and cigarettes was because everybody else did. God really blessed me, because over the years I never developed a strong habit like some of my friends did. Whether it was wine, pills, reefer—I never got addicted. It's said that God looks out for babies and fools, and I was both during the period of my life when I was into drug experimentation.

The Seventh-Day Adventist religion was so doggone restrictive that I never gave it a chance as a kid. I've already mentioned that from sundown Friday until sundown Saturday, Seventh-Day Adventists can't do anything. You can't read a book, play with toys, or even work at your job. My mother was an exception to that last rule because she provided health care, and that is one of the few types of work that Seventh-Day Adventists are allowed to engage in during the Sabbath.

Our church was in a working-class part of town that eventually became dilapidated. The church was located about two miles from Prairie Street, on Grand River Street, one of Detroit's major thoroughfares.

I clashed with the church on a number of levels, not the least of which had to do with clothes. I wanted to step into church looking smooth and sharp, enabling me to profile for the cute girls there. However, the church wanted young people to wear phony-looking, preppy type stuff. The end result was that I rolled into church decked out in long-sleeved shirts that made me look like a square white boy in a JCPenney catalog.

Don't think my boys on Prairie Street, and later Herman Gardens, didn't notice, either. The minute I walked out the door on Saturday to go to church, they'd start clowning on me. Hard. "Yo, what kind of shit he wearing?" "Man, I tole you he ain't nothin' but a PUNK! Ha, ha, ha, ha, ha."

It wasn't as if I had a choice in the matter—Mama made it crystal clear: "If you live in my house, you have to go to church."

From the time I was a baby, all of my Friday nights were spent inside the Seventh-Day Adventist church. Friday nights were really hard on me, because that was when my crew went to parties and generally hung out. My Saturdays were spoken for, too, starting with a Bible class that began at eight A.M and lasted until one P.M. Then I would return for the Saturday afternoon service, which began at five P.M. and ended at eight P.M.

I got into fights at church and also stole stuff out of the choir members' coats once they'd trekked upstairs to practice. To remedy this, my mother used to make me sit beside her on her pew as soon as we walked in the church door. She would put me right up under her to make sure I wasn't laughing and joking around. If I did, she would pinch me so hard that I was convinced the flesh was coming off my bony arms and legs.

Looking back, I marvel at my ability to get into mischief while at church, because Mama used to watch me like a hawk. Plus the deacons at my church were basically frustrated prison guards.

"Where are you going, young Mr. Mathis?"

"I'm going to the bathroom!"

"You just *went* to the bathroom."

I would screw up my face during those exchanges, but I actually enjoyed them. Because even though I felt stifled in the Seventh-Day Adventist environment, I also felt a lot of love emanating from it. It was clear to me that the adults in the church school, and in the church itself, genuinely cared about me. Anybody who tells you that's not a gratifying feeling when you're a child, or when you're an adult, is a damned liar.

Sure, there were snooty kids in the church who snubbed me, but by and large it was a place where I felt secure.

Something else I liked about church was that it had a lot of activities for young people. There were socials on Saturday night after the sun went down, as well as skating parties. But it was understood that you weren't going to get any coochie from those Seventh-Day Adventist girls. Their stuff was under lock and key.

My first sexual encounter took place when I was a first-grader and it consisted of being buck naked and humping against some girls who were also naked.

All the grunting and thrusting felt good, but I didn't have the foggiest idea how to get my penis into the promised land. So all we did was hump. I didn't come up with a solution to that problem until I was twelve years old.

I was in junior high school and cut class with a girlfriend whom I was pressuring to have sex. I was constantly hearing my brothers and my boys (most of whom were probably lying through their teeth) wax poetic about doing the nasty, so I was intent on following suit.

Me and this girl went to a house near our school where a youthful occupant always let kids come in and drink, smoke weed, and get busy when they should have been in class getting educated.

That first encounter was very difficult for me and for my partner, because she was a virgin, too. It didn't help matters that I wore a condom, even though I had never ejaculated in my life. But hey, the big boys used them so I figured I needed one, too.

That condom merely guaranteed that my girlfriend and I would have a miserable liaison.

Instead of making me swear off sex, I just resolved to do it again with a girl who was a nonvirgin. The best way to pull that off was to follow one of my brothers to the "bad girls' home." That's what we called the Barrett House, which was an establishment for troubled girls who had been removed from their homes, then placed in a residential setting. It's a nonprofit that receives funding from the city and state. Years later, when I worked for Detroit's city council, I assisted it in getting funding.

However, during my reprobate years, the Barrett House was a clearinghouse of easy pussy. It had anywhere from thirty to forty girls in it, and their hormones were usually ablaze, just like those of their teenage male counterparts.

You didn't need much in the way of rap, and you didn't need to blow a lot of money to get over at the Barrett House. Nor did you have to sit around and bullshit with some girl's mama or daddy.

You might have to give one of those Barrett House girls a dollar or two or buy 'em an ice cream. That was all it took to get them to sneak out of the place and into the car of some young brother.

My brother Ron was never in on this, because he was out of the house and attending the University of Detroit by that time. So it would be me sitting on the couch, listening as Rick and Kenny orchestrated their Barrett House visits.

When Kenny turned eighteen he bought a car, a shiny, dark blue Plymouth Duster. Man, it was on then! That Duster could have been called the Barrett House Express!

Before that, we were riding with Kenny's buddies who had cars and who never wanted me around. Among other things, they noted that I never paid for gas, which was true. Plus, I was annoying, manipulative, outtalked them, and outsmarted them. Whatever they were doing, I thought I could do it better.

Kenny and his crew were at an age when they were going after girls, which was another reason they were keen on ditching me. Naturally I couldn't wait to go with them, especially to the Barrett House.

"Are we gonna take them girls to a hotel, or do it in the backseat?"

"Yo, man, I got twenty dollars. Wanna get a room?"

"Solid. Let's head on over to the bad girls' house."

I had to hear about these visits over and over, tortured by the graphic details my brothers spilled later. Nothing was going to keep me from making it to the bad girls' house. I nagged Rick and Kenny so bad that they finally took me.

The first time, I was just an observer. After the girls came outside and went over to Kenny's car, they saw me sitting in the backseat and exclaimed: "Why you got this little boy with you?" They patted me on the head—though not the head I wanted them to pat—and talked about how "cute" I was.

During that visit to the Barrett House, I sat in the backseat of Kenny's car being cute, while my brother got all the action. I swore I wasn't going to let that happen again.

Our next visit took place on a night when just me and Kenny were in the car. He went to a window of the bad girls' house, because he wasn't allowed inside, and starting talking to a girl leaning out the window. After a few minutes a brown-skinned girl who was cute and kind of thick came outside. The young sister, who looked to be about fifteen, was supposed to be my partner for the night.

Of course Kenny also came back with a girl for himself. He drove to a hotel, parked the car, and left with his companion to rent a room. My girl and I were supposed to wait for him to get back, then we would be able to use the room, too. But I guess it started getting good to Kenny, because he didn't return after quite some time.

So me and that little brown-skinned cutie took care of business in the backseat of Kenny's car. She was soft and didn't smell like she had paid an awful lot of attention to personal hygiene. Some deodorant definitely would have been in order. Despite that, I enjoyed myself and after a while I got to be a regular on those nightly runs. My brother told me that I was just wasting condoms when I used them, so I stopped wearing them. Unfortunately that practice tripped me up after I turned thirteen, because one of the kids from the bad girls' house gave me a case of the claps.

I had known since I was seven years old that having sex was how babies were made. Another boy who lived in the Herman Gardens projects, Ricky Wells, had broken that down for me in no uncertain terms. But no one had ever told me anything linking sex to painful urination and a greenish discharge. My dick was stinging like a son of a bitch. I told my brothers and friends, "Man, I got some creamy shit that keeps running out the head of my dick. Do you know what that is?"

"Oh shit, oh shit—man, you got a case of the claps!"

I was like, "Yeah!" because contracting gonorrhea was a badge of honor for me. There could be no doubt among my brothers and my peers that I was really getting pussy if I had the claps.

But it doesn't take long for the novelty to burn off when your dick feels like a forest fire is raging inside it every time you go to the bathroom. My pride turned into concern, and eventually panic. Because I knew I would have to confront my mother with my problem.

Which is exactly what happened.

"Mama, I think I need to go to the doctor. It burns when I pee."

She had to drive me down to the city health department, and the ride seemed like it lasted for two days. The radio was turned off and the only sound in Mama's car was her fussing at me, which she did during the entire trip. Part of her wrath was directed at me, but the brunt of it focused on Kenny.

"Y'all supposed to be supervising this boy," she mumbled. "I'm working two jobs to take care of everybody, and this is what you damn fools do while I'm gone?"

After a health department doctor had me pull my trousers down and administered a painful silver bullet to my backside, Mama drove me back home and delivered another tongue lashing that seemed to last another two days.

I actually managed to block out some of her tirade, because by the time I was thirteen I was getting chastised and fussed at on average four or five days a week about something I was doing. I could deal with the beatings, too, but what I couldn't stand was when my mother would get so fed up with me that she would start crying.

Her tears hurt me worse than any beating or tirade, although not to the point where they made me permanently mend my ways.

Mama had good reason to weep, because I had been arrested for theft and gone to juvenile court when I was twelve years old. There's no question that I was pushing the thug lifestyle to the absolute limit.

I'll tell you why—me and a couple other members of my crew lived in households that were dominated by the Seventh-Day Adventists. All of us disappeared from Friday afternoon until Saturday at sundown, because we were imprisoned in church all that time.

So the other guys we ran with viewed us with suspicion, figuring we naturally had to be soft. I couldn't stand being seen that way.

I became the crazy MF who would shoot at someone or stab or go off in a heartbeat. Once you earn your rep in the streets, people know not to fuck with you anymore.

Not only that, but you gotta maintain your rep in school, too. That hadn't been a problem at Peterson, where I and another student named Andre were the twin scourges. Originally, we had been criminal rivals at Peterson, but after talking it over decided it made sense to join forces instead of competing against each other. We had a pact: He would rifle the lockers at one end of a hallway while I stood lookout, then we'd reverse roles. One day I was taking shit out of lockers like it was going out of style, while Andre was supposed to be watching my back.

Not very well, though, because the principal—big ass Mr. Bradford—came strolling down the hall and caught me in the act. Without Andre so much as saying boo! How could you not see someone as gargantuan as Mr. Bradford creeping down the hall unless you didn't want to?

Since it looked like I had been set up, I told Mr. Bradford that Andre was in on it, too.

He took both of us to the office and questioned us about our locker thefts. Students had been complaining that things were turning up missing from their lockers, so the principal was delighted to have rolled up on Andre and me.

We both got suspended for a couple of days, but that wasn't the worst part. Before Mr. Bradford would allow us to return, we both had to apologize to the entire school for our misdeeds.

I wasn't that keen on apologizing or returning to school, but Mama made it crystal clear that was exactly what I had to do. She had spanked me so fiercely that I knew damn well she wasn't playing, either.

So I returned to Peterson, with my head held high. The Great Confession was to take place in the school auditorium during a prayer gathering that took place once a week. I've told you that I don't like to appear weak, and that's exactly how I was going to look after standing before the entire student body and apologizing. I was going to look like the biggest punk who'd ever entered Peterson's doors. But there was no way around it, so at the appointed time I took a microphone into my sweaty hands and looked out over hundreds of pairs of taunting, mocking eyes. I felt a little embarrassment, but mainly an incandescent rage at Mr. Bradford and all the students smirking at me.

"I apologize for breaking into your lockers and stealing y'all's stuff," I quickly mumbled into the mic, then swaggered back to my seat, shooting a death stare at anyone stupid enough to make eye contact with me.

Later on, my behavior got so bad that my brother Ron pulled me up and warned me that I needed to stop fucking up and making things tough for Mama. Instead of making much of an impression on me, to my way of thinking he just became another authority figure I had to work around. Anyway, he was off at college most of the time and rarely home, so why was I going to worry about him?

III

SEARS HAS EVERYTHING

Thanks to Kenny's blue Plymouth Duster, I was spending less and less time around Herman Gardens or Prairie Street.

Instead, I was usually up to no good with Kenny and Rick, who today is my closest friend. He grew up in the Brewster projects that produced Diana Ross and Joe Louis.

Rick's older brother, Mike, was a heroin dealer for whom Rick did little odd jobs like carrying a package here and there. It's a good thing Rick wasn't too heavily involved in his brother's drug enterprise, because Mike was constantly in and out of jail. Whenever he got released, his money would always be funny, and we would turn to street crime to generate a little scratch for him.

Our usual modus operandi was to engage in purse snatchings, which we never committed in our own community. For the most part we victimized white suburbs like Dearborn and Southfield.

Kenny and I were at Herman Gardens one day when Rick came over and said that Mike wanted to make a move. The plan was to hit a Sears store in Westland, a predominantly white suburb. Since I was thirteen and had done my share of shakedowns and snatch-and-grabs, I demanded to be included in the action.

Kenny was aware that I was streetwise and a budding thug in my own right, but he still took a couple of minutes to think about whether I should go. "Okay little muthafucka, come on!" he finally said grudgingly.

Kenny, Rick, and I left Herman Gardens to go hook up with Mike, who wasn't exactly thrilled to see me. He frowned, gave Kenny and Rick a look like they had lost their minds, and then pointed in my general direction. "Whatcha doin' with him, man?" Mike demanded in his gravely heroin voice.

"He ain't gonna do nothin', Mike. He's just gonna walk around Sears and be our lookout, that's all," Kenny said without hesitation. I stuck out my chest a little bit, proud that Kenny had that much trust and faith in me.

It never even occurred to me that we might be apprehended. The prevailing thought in my mind was that I was *never* gonna get caught. That's what most criminals believe; otherwise they wouldn't do what they do.

We set out to pull off our Sears caper. We had a stolen van that Kenny drove to Westland and parked in the Sears parking lot. The first thing we did inside the store was get a silver shopping cart, then quickly roll it into the hardware section and put a garbage can in it. Then we put a hammer and a hatchet in the cart, too.

At first I didn't know what those guys had in mind, but the heist started to make sense when Kenny, Rick, and Mike pushed the shopping cart into the menswear section and started snatching expensive two- and three-piece suits off the racks and tossing them into the garbage can. After shoplifting about eight suits, we headed into womenswear and boosted a similar number of dresses.

They did all this very calmly, mind you, with the nonchalance of any other shopper in the store. I admired the cool way they went about their work.

With the trash can bulging, they slowly pushed the cart toward the front of the store, past the people waiting in line at the cash register and toward the front door.

A white male security guard was near the front of the store and he immediately began to approach us with a suspicious look on his face. None of us exactly looked like Sears's typical Westland clientele.

Acting as innocent as could be, I sped up and intercepted the guard. I was carrying a pair of socks that I had stolen and, not surprisingly, boosted candy.

"Where's the bathroom at, mister?" I asked out of the blue, as another security guard came in our general direction from the rear of the store. As this was taking place, my three partners in crime were steadily creeping up behind me.

"Are those things paid for?" the first guard asked gruffly, looking at my insignificant items. Which is precisely what I wanted him to concentrate on.

"YEAH, they're paid for," I said in a loud, indignant voice. "What you frontin' on me for, man? I just came to ask you where the bathroom was!" On cue, my crew pulled out the hatchet and hammer they stole out of hardware and started swinging them around like madmen.

Those two security guards could have qualified for an Olympic track and field event, they jetted toward the back of the store so fast.

We got away from Sears safely and wasted no time selling our deeply discounted suits and dresses to bargain-conscious shoppers back at Herman Gardens. When I was given fifty dollars for my role in the Sears caper, I distinctly remember thinking: This is the life! This is how you make big money—this is what I want to do.

It was 1973, and at thirteen I had hit upon the formula for generating significant wealth.

I was going to use my fifty dollars to buy some weed and sell it. Then I would turn around and use those profits to buy some nice clothes, which would allow me to become a big-time pimp.

I had it all figured out. Only problem was, that fifty dollars burned a hole in my pocket. I spent it pretty quickly, so it was back to the drawing board.

Our scams took Kenny and me downtown quite a bit. We

frequently ran into members of Detroit's top gang, the Errol Flynns. The moniker came from the movie star of the same name, who was swashbuckling and classy but was still a thug. The Flynns had declared downtown their turf, but the little operations I was involved in were so small that I wasn't considered a threat.

The Errol Flynns were primarily into robberies and snatch-and-grabs. They also spent a lot of time fighting rival gang members. But the wars didn't result in the kind of senseless slaughter that you see today when inner-city gangs tangle. Back then, guns weren't as easy to get as they are today, so a rumble was usually limited to a physical altercation.

Encountering the Errol Flynns put me in touch with a whole new universe that I found fascinating. They had style with their fancy suits and hundred-dollar Borsalino hats. They bopped through the downtown area carrying canes, umbrellas, briefcases, wearing glass-heeled shoes and big white glasses, a style of eyewear made popular by musician George Clinton.

Most of the Errol Flynns were teenagers, but a few members were in their twenties. There were a number of Errol Flynn crews throughout the city, and their leader was an older guy named Big Keith, who was a loud, very threatening guy.

I may have admired the Errol Flynns, but I never wanted to be like Big Keith—I always wanted to be smoother, like the pimps and hustlers. Since it was summer, and there was no school, I had quite a bit of time to be in their company.

Although I wasn't quite in the same league as the Errol Flynns, I was starting to pull off more sophisticated capers that brought in bigger and bigger payoffs.

During the summer of 1973, two of my partners and I set our sights on robbing a jewelry store in downtown Detroit. We were going to do a smash-and-grab, meaning our modus operandi would be to shatter the glass in one of the store's display cases, snatch whatever jewelry was present, and scamper out the door.

When the day dawned for pulling off our heist, we went over our plan one final time, then piled into a car and headed for downtown Detroit. As we rode to our destination, I enjoyed an incredible rush that boosted me so high I was nearly giddy. The closest thing I can compare it to is the excitement and anticipation you feel before having sex.

I was the first one to enter the store and immediately distracted a salesman by asking him to show me a ring in one of the display counters. One of my partners had another salesperson show him a necklace, while our third accomplice kind of loitered around, pretending to browse and admire jewelry.

The three of us wore baseball caps and conservative eyeglasses, which in retrospect wasn't much of a disguise.

After we'd been in the store about three minutes, my buddy who had been "admiring" things smashed one of the display cases with a hammer and grabbed some diamond jewelry. All three of us hauled ass out of the store to the street where we had parked a car.

Definitely a low-tech, high-risk operation, but it went off without a hitch. One of the worst things that can happen to a criminal is to have a crime go off like clockwork, without any complications. Repeated success starts to make you believe that you're incapable of making mistakes.

That was my mind-set one sunshine-filled day as I set out to do a little purse-snatching at a Kmart about a mile and a half from Herman Gardens with David and Robert, my two buddies from church. They lived in the Herman Gardens projects and were going down the same path I was streaking along at breakneck speed.

We went to Kmart in the car of Keith Timmons, who was four years older than us and had a reputation for being wild and crazy. I don't know what we were thinking, because we all looked like suspects as we rode to the Kmart store.

The building had a five-foot-tall brick wall behind it. The game plan was to snatch a purse, run to the back of the Kmart, and then hop over the wall.

Keith dropped me off in the parking lot in front of the store, then drove around to the rear and parked behind the brick wall with his engine running. That's because Kmart had taken to having security vehicles patrol its parking lot. They were responding to purse snatchings and thefts of car radios, performed by little hardheads just like me.

Before I hopped out of the car, I looked at my three buddies, who were grinning and otherwise looking quite unconcerned. Just another day at the office. I, on the other hand, was practically vibrating from all the adrenaline circulating in my system. I would need that energy to wrest a pocketbook from the first white woman I encountered, then fly like the wind to the rear of the store.

"See you guys around back," I mumbled.

"Yeah, man. Don't go for no poor-looking bitch, okay?"

Laughing, my boys glided off toward the rear of the store, the Temptations blaring from the radio.

I walked through the hot asphalt parking lot at a leisurely pace, to give Keith enough time to make it to the rear of the store. As I got closer to the front door, I spied a frumpy, middle-aged white woman standing on the sidewalk in front of the Kmart, carelessly dangling her pocketbook in her left hand. Her back was turned to me as she looked at something inside the store. Probably waiting for a friend.

It didn't matter whether she turned around or not, because I felt enough power coursing through my body to rip her arm off if she tried to resist. It wasn't in my mind to hurt that woman, but I had no problem doing whatever it took to get her pocketbook.

Before swooping in for the kill, I looked left and right, making sure no rent-a-cops or potential Good Samaritans were in the vicinity. The coast was clear—nobody was paying me any attention.

Still walking with a casual gait, I approached the woman, grabbed her pocketbook, and yanked it with all my might. By the time she figured out what was happening, I was already streaking at full speed toward the rear of the store, pounding the pavement with my Converse sneakers.

"Hey—HEY! He's got my purse," the woman shrieked as I rounded the corner, moving at a breakneck pace toward the five-foot-high brick wall. Still at a dead run, I leaped into the air about three feet from the wall, skinning my knee as I grabbed the top of the wall and hauled myself over, my precious cargo clutched in my right hand.

Before I had time to settle into my seat, Keith was gunning the engine and getting us away from that Kmart as quickly as possible. I had done it again! I laughed as I slapped my boys five and started sorting through that woman's belongings.

We had taken a small amount of cash from the pocketbook and tossed it out the car window when a police car pulled up behind us, lights flashing and siren blaring. Some eagle-eyed witness had identified our car.

"Oh shit, man!" Keith muttered, peering into his rearview mirror. "Check this shit out!"

The cops quickly surrounded his car, their guns drawn, looking tense. "I want all of you to get out, get down on the ground, and put your hands on your head," one of the cops said in a booming voice. "Slowly! You snatched a purse, you little motherfuckers."

"You ain't got shit on us," one of my partners snarled as we crept out of Keith's car. I wasn't saying a damn thing myself, because I figured that if the purse-snatching victim could identify anyone, it would be me.

Plus I was the only one sweating from having sprinted away from the Kmart.

The cops took us down to a juvenile holding facility that smelled like a musty locker room. After me and my boys got fingerprinted, we were put in a lineup. I'm sure I looked anxious as I stood there, squinting from the bright lights shining in my face. I knew that white woman was on the other side of a one-way mirror on the wall, eyeballing me and my boys. I imagined her eyes boring into my face, as she triumphantly told the cops, "There he is. There's the little black bastard!"

Doing my best to maintain a poker face, I envisioned my fate: Because of my age, in all likelihood I would probably go to a juvenile detention center instead of jail. Based on everything that I had heard, juvenile detention centers were a piece of cake. You just went to school, then spent the rest of the day in a dormitory-like setting.

So I figured what the hell—I can do that standing on my head. Plus, I hadn't been getting that much pussy anyway, so it wasn't as though I would be hit hard in that area.

That's what was going through my mind as I stood with four other black males ranging in age from early teens to late twenties, listening to a white police officer bark directions about where to stand and which way to turn. But fortunately that woman couldn't manage to identify me.

When they told me I was free to go, I couldn't believe my good fortune. All I had to do now was call Mama and have her come get me out. I was smirking as a cop handed me the phone to make a phone call.

"Hey, Mama."

"Greg, it's late. Where are you?"

"Mama, the cops took me down to the juvenile detention center, but I ain't done nothin'. I swear it! They even said I ain't done nothin' and they ain't gonna charge me. Mama, please come and get me."

"Where did you say you were again?" my mother asked in a voice several octaves higher than before.

"I'm down at juvie, Mama, but they won't let me go 'less you come and get me."

"Who were you with? Keith?"

"Uh-huh."

"You know better than to hang out with Keith. Y'all know better than to hang out with that boy. Don't call me with this foolishness—stay down there until you rot!" *Click.*

I just stared at the phone, flabbergasted. I couldn't believe my mother had hung up on me.

I didn't know that Mama had called Robert's mother afterward and asked her to pick me up. I freaked out until Robert's mom came and got me.

When I knocked on the door of my apartment, Steve pulled it open with a half grin on his face. Behind him in the living room, I could see the evil-looking visage of my mother. She was sitting in a chair and had a death grip on two leather belts that were folded so that the metal buckle was enclosed in her hand.

"I ain't done nothin', let me go!" I squealed at Steve, who grabbed me to prevent me from escaping. "What I need a whippin' for? The police harass everybody around here!"

"You shouldn't have been with Keith," Mama growled as she slowly rose from the chair. "You know better. What were you doing riding with Keith in his car when you were supposed to have been at the portico?"

At that point I broke away from Steve and dashed into the bedroom Kenny and I shared. I broke into a baseball slide and my momentum carried me way up under my bed, far enough so that my back was against the wall.

Seeing that her belts were now useless, Mama went and got the broom and a mop handle. She used them to poke me in the ribs and in my head while I was under the bed. She did it hard, too. Mama only needed a few minutes of that to flush her prey into the open, where her belts could finish the job.

"I . . . am . . . so . . . tired . . . of . . . this," my mother said, pausing after each word as she took vicious roundhouse swings that sent agonizing jolts through my back, butt, and legs. That's where the blows landed as long as I remained reasonably still, but if I tried to run or twist out of the way I got hit wherever the belt happened to land.

I will never steal from Kmart again and I'm not going to steal any more purses, I promised myself after Mama gave me the worst beating of my life. From now on I'm going to hit other stores, and I'm only going to steal things I ain't gonna get caught boosting, I thought to myself.

Once I was able to reunite with my boys, I flaunted my brief visit to juvenile detention like it was a badge of honor. I told war stories about juvie like the old heads told horror stories about going to the state pen. Getting arrested and not being charged had proved to be a boon to my reputation.

And true to my promise to myself, I didn't steal anything else from Kmart. However, whenever Mama came into my room, she noticed the little knickknacks I'd been buying with my ill-gotten gains.

"Greg, where are you getting the money from to buy these clothes and snacks?"

I brushed off her questions by saying that I had been mowing lawns or bagging groceries.

My mother was no fool, though. Feeling that she had run out of options in her quest to make me walk the straight and narrow, Mama finally threw up her hands and sent me to live with my father on Detroit's rough-and-tumble East Side.

IV

LIFE WITH DAD

When Mama told me she was tired of my antics and was sending me off to live with my father, it was probably one of the first times I felt a little fear. He lived in a particularly gritty East Side neighborhood that was old and dilapidated. It had a lot more drug addicts, drunks, street people, and crime than even Herman Gardens.

I'd met my father maybe twice and from what I'd heard, he had a little street in him, too. Was he going to try and fight me and come down on me hard? I'd seen plenty of fathers around the projects beating their sons with their fists, or pulling out pistols and pistol-whipping them.

I also wondered how long it would take to earn my rep on the East Side, so I could keep folks off my ass. I decided that the best way to handle the situation was to go over there and immediately do something crazy.

My father owned a run-down East Side building that contained a storefront church his wife ran. Actually, he'd never married Mother Mathis, who was a nice middle-aged woman who was overweight and reminded me a little bit of my mother.

Mother Mathis was into spirituality and the church thing, which was okay with me. As far as I was concerned, it would just be more of the same. But I would later come to find out that she was about as genuine as a three-dollar bill.

Opposite the church on the first floor of my dad's building was a greasy spoon restaurant that he operated. The upstairs section of the building was divided into two halves. On one side were living quarters, on the other a flea market/secondhand store. Outside was a lunar landscape of dilapidated buildings and vacant lots that served as a haven for menacing brown rats that had absolutely no fear of humans.

When my mother dropped me off at my father's place, I distinctly remember going into the restaurant and sitting down by myself as my parents went into a back room to talk. The place smelled of cooking odors and everything in it had a cheesy, secondhand quality.

Charles Mathis was a balding, dark-complexioned man who wasn't particularly handsome, had a big round nose, and stood about five-foot-ten. I didn't see much of myself in him.

There were no hugs or embraces during our encounter. Instead of having a father-to-son conversation with me—which I needed—my father came off as brusque and cold.

"Your mom tells me you're having problems over there," he said matter-of-factly. "Well, it's gonna be a different ball game over here, 'cause I ain't raising no babies. You got to be a man over here. You can work in this restaurant with me and carry your own weight."

I studied my father, not sure what to make of him. He was interacting with me more on a street macho tip, the way street guys interact with each other, than as father. There was nothing warm or nurturing about the way he talked to me.

My immediate impression was that living with my pops was going to be a good thing, because it looked as though he was going to let me do my own thing and treat me like the man I already thought I was at thirteen.

Hopefully he would let me come and go as I pleased and I would have some money in my pocket from working in his little restaurant.

It didn't take long to get a taste of what working in his restaurant was all about. I think I started that first day.

I cleaned floors and bused tables, definitely alien behavior for me. Waiting on customers was novel for the first two or three times I did it, but it got old quickly. Needless to say, tips were practically nonexistent.

I hadn't been in the restaurant long before I noticed that quite a few Errol Flynn gang members seemed to be regular customers.

They would usually enter lugging merchandise, often meat and new clothes, then would disappear into a back room with my father. When they reappeared, they were always empty-handed. It didn't take me long to figure out what was going on: My old man was fencing for the Flynns!

I eagerly befriended the Errol Flynns who came into my father's place and once I had finished my duties mopping the floor and waiting on tables, I would drink wine and smoke reefer with them.

When my father saw that I was falling in with the gang, he didn't seem perturbed at all. His attitude was like, Okay, you're on your own now, if this is what you want to do. Watch your back!

So I no longer had to sneak around and could basically do as I damn well pleased. Thank you, Mama, for dropping me off at my father's to get straightened out!

Curious to see how her little experiment was going, she called me at least once a week to keep tabs on things.

"How are things working out, Greg?" Mama would ask in a concerned voice.

"Everything's fine. I'm just working, that's all."

"You keeping the Sabbath?"

"Yeah, Mama, I'm keeping the Sabbath."

Given my history, I don't know why my mother believed that last lie. But she was probably so sick of me at that point that as long as my father wasn't torturing me, she had no problem with me staying right where I was.

For the first time in my life, being Charles Mathis's offspring actually conferred some status upon me and I got a kick out of that. Among the Flynns, I was "Mathis's boy." Meaning I didn't have to make a rep for myself by playing crazy, because nobody fucked with me.

It took me only a matter of days to see that everybody in the household was running a scam of one kind or another. I saw that Mother Mathis was passing herself off as a prophet, a seer who could tell you what the winning numbers were or ascertain what a woman's wayward husband was up to.

My father and his common-law wife were straight-up hustlers, no two ways about it. Mother Mathis would give you the number, then you could go see old man Mathis for whatever stolen goods you might need.

Mother Mathis made a big show of lavishing affection on me, but her actions were all fake.

"Oh baby, you need anything, baby? Come here to Mother Mathis, baby. Now you know if you run into anybody who needs the number, send them to Mother Mathis!"

Everything that came out of her mouth was con, including her show of love for me. She played the church con—that was her game.

Within five days after I arrived at my father's I got my first gun, a .38-caliber, long-handle pistol that I kept tucked in my pants. One of the Flynns got it for me, and I went into the back room in my father's restaurant and admired it for a good half hour. It was a little heavier than I thought it would be, and it had scratches on its barrel and a couple of nicks on its wooden handle. After studying my weapon with something approaching reverence, I alternately placed it in one of my pant pockets or my waistband and practiced quick drawing it like a Wild West gunslinger.

I always wanted a gun because it gave you the power to take a life or spare a life. It wasn't a question of whether I needed a gun; no thirteen-year-old living in a big city does. I just wanted it.

I reveled in the lifestyle I was living at my father's place. The two of us didn't have much of a relationship, but being able to run with members of the Errol Flynn gang more than made up for that.

For a month and a half I did whatever I felt like doing. My Errol Flynn–running buddies and I were big on doing house burglaries, primarily to see if we could find any handguns. We also broke into some gun stores, using wire cutters and other tools.

Another favorite target was jewelry stores, where we would snatch and grab rings and bracelets and whatever else we could get our hands on. We usually did those in Detroit's suburbs, where the nicest jewelry was sold.

All good things come to an end, however, and my downfall was brought about by a member of my mother's church who spied me hanging out with the Errol Flynns on an East Side street one afternoon. But this nosy busybody couldn't leave it at that—she investigated a little further and found out that the Flynns hung out at my Dad's restaurant.

That was the beginning of the end of life with Father. My mother came flying into my father's restaurant one day, scowling like nobody's business. My brother Kenny was with Mama, too, and not looking real happy to be along for the trip.

As I've mentioned before, my mother almost never cussed, except for a "damn" and a "shit" every blue moon. She was cussing up a storm that day, though.

"Where your damn daddy at?" she spat out as soon as she walked through the front door of his business. "I send your ass over here, and he has you runnin' around and cuttin' up like a damned hoodlum. He's turned you into a bigger hoodlum. Where's he at?"

"He's in the back, Mom. I'll go get him."

"Naw, you ain't gotta go get nothin'. Shit!"

She went into the back room where my father was and lit into him. I couldn't hear exactly what she was saying, but I did hear her curse words piercing the air. And I heard my father respond with a laugh that sounded defensive, as he desperately tried to get a word in edgewise.

"Huh—whatchoo talkin' about, woman? I'm trying to get this boy some work. Why you trippin'?"

The conversation didn't last long, because Mama stalked out of the back room. She scooped me up, gathered my possessions, and stuffed me into her car. Then we hightailed it out of there, headed back to Herman Gardens.

Frankly, I was relieved. Because I felt a little lonely and unloved and uncared for. And I had felt myself gradually becoming a lot more callous and wilder and had an unsettling feeling that I was on the verge of going to a place I might not be able to return from.

I didn't care about anyone or anything anymore, and that bothered me a little bit. I used to care when I hurt people, but when I went over to my father's place I didn't give a damn about anything, because I felt like nobody cared about me. It wasn't a good feeling.

I felt more hostile toward society, because I didn't feel any love from anywhere. When I was with my mother I felt love from her and from the church surroundings. But with my father, everything was ice cold. His unspoken take on life was, It's a tough-ass world out here and it's all about survival of the fittest. So don't come to me with no mushy stuff—I ain't showing you no love and I ain't looking for no love from you.

V

"MISS MATHIS, WHERE ARE YOU?"

When I got back to Herman Gardens, I returned preaching the gospel of the Errol Flynns and wasn't shy about letting everybody know that I had been running with them.

"Hey, man, I'm an Errol Flynn, and we need to be Errol Flynns now."

So me and my little crew started pulling off Errol Flynn–type moves. It was as though I had gone off and gotten a master's degree in petty crime during the six weeks I was with my father.

In the time-honored tradition of each one, teach one, I taught six of my running buddies all there was to know about breaking and entering and how to run snatch-and-grabs. Vending machines cringed when they saw us coming, because we were always taking a baseball bat or crowbar to them. If we managed to get a cold soda pop or a candy bar out of the deal, then we really felt like we'd hit the jackpot!

One thing that was never in my repertoire, though, was car theft. I've never stolen one in my life because I am not the least bit mechanically inclined. I can't screw in a lightbulb without breaking it.

Though I had become even more streetwise during my stay at my dad's house, Mama didn't notice much of a change in me. That's

because when I was around her, I was still the same as I had been before I left.

When I was around my crew, on the other hand, the corners of my
mouth would be turned down and my head would be cocked to the
side. With them, my speech was taken over by "you dig?" and "you
unnerstan'?" and "what up?"

Around my mother, I had a perky *Leave It to Beaver* persona going
on—"Hi, Mama! Can I have some more Jell-O, please, Mama? Kenny
took my stuff, Mama!"

I would have a new world to deal with shortly, because the summer was rapidly slipping away and it was time to return to school. I
went back to Peterson, where I shook down those bourgeois black
kids and broke into their lockers just for the hell of it. You might think
I would have stopped that after having been humiliated in front of the
entire school. But I had gotten to the point where I needed more than
respect from my peers at Peterson. I needed to be feared, I needed to
be able to shoot somebody a hard glance and have them dig into their
pocket to pay me off.

The reason I was so good at generating fear in folks is because fear
and intimidation ruled the day at Herman Gardens. Among the boys
in the neighborhood, a popular pastime was to catch a cat and hang
it by the neck from the clothesline near the portico. Then somebody
would douse the hapless feline with lighter fluid and set it ablaze. This
was great sport among a few of my neighbors.

I remember the first time I saw this horrible spectacle played out.
A good-sized tan-colored cat was screeching like crazy and clawing at
its captor, who had the poor animal by the neck and was dancing and
writhing to avoid the desperate feline's claws and teeth. Streaks of
bright red blood began to appear on the young executioner's arms as
he sprayed a steady stream of colorless lighter fluid on his dripping-
wet victim. Some of the fluid got into the animal's eyes and it really
began to go wild, flopping and thrashing about in a frantic bid to free
itself of the clothesline.

I watched dumbstruck, secretly feeling sorry for the cat and dying to rescue it. There's always been a side of my personality that roots for, and protects, underdogs. Being a thug isn't necessarily synonymous with being a sadist.

However, I observed unspoken code at the portico the day that cat was dispatched to the great litter box in the sky; I couldn't risk doing or saying anything hinting of disapproval.

A match was finally lit and that cat became a squirming fireball. I'll never forget two things about that day—the horrible sound that came from that animal's lungs once the flames started eating at it, and the disgusting smell from its burning hair and flesh.

"Damn!" I exclaimed to no one in particular.

Several of the neighborhood boys turned away from the spectacle to momentarily glance at me. "Whatchoo, a punk or somethin'?" one boy sneered. "A bitch?"

Looking back on it, I think burning cats was a part of their soul-hardening ritual. If you live in a cold, unforgiving environment, you can't afford to run around being compassionate and soft-hearted. When that happens, your environment eats you alive.

Herman Gardens had gotten to be so crime-ridden that my mother had to be escorted to her car when she left for Henry Ford Hospital at night.

Heroin junkies had overrun our housing project and were snatching residents' purses and pulling stick-ups to get that next fix. Because of this, my brothers usually walked Mama the one hundred or so feet that it took to get from our unit to the trash-littered parking lot, but one bitterly cold fall night in October 1974, none of my brothers were home. I was there with one of my friends, so Mama ordered me to look out the window and keep an eye on her as she went to her car.

She casually strolled out of my line of sight, but at that point she only had an additional twenty feet or so to walk. I watched her moving toward her vehicle, impatient for her to pull off so my friend and I could get outside and start running some hustles.

About five minutes later, as we were about to make our move,

Steve came rushing into our apartment, looking anxious and breathing hard, like he'd been running.

"Where Mama at? Where Mama?" Steve blurted. I felt an immediate sensation of dread in my stomach.

"She already gone, man. Y'all late. She's already gone to work—she left ten minutes ago."

"Well, her car still out there."

"Maybe she stopped at somebody's house?"

The three of us decided to go outside and stand beside Mama's car until she appeared from wherever she had gone. I had a bad feeling, because Mama was so dependable and so predictable that something had to be terribly wrong for her to alter her routine.

When Mama didn't show up after fifteen minutes, we started knocking on apartment doors around Herman Gardens, asking if anybody had seen her. Every time we got a negative response my anxiety pegged a little higher, taking me closer and closer to panic. I had often thought that something could happen to me or my brothers, but I never imagined that anything bad could happen to Mama.

Not only was she the foundation of our family, but to my young mind she was indestructible.

Eventually Steve and I rounded up a posse and we went all over the grounds of Herman Gardens, looking behind every Dumpster and under every bush. If Mama was anywhere on the premises, we were going to find her.

Soon cries of "Miss Mathis, Miss Mathis!" were ringing through the housing project. Talk about surreal. As we walked around scouring the place and calling out my mother's name, some unkempt bushes not far from our apartment unit suddenly quivered, as if someone had pushed them.

"Hey, here in the bushes! Come check this out, man!"

About thirty of us converged on the hedges, where a member of the search party was frantically pointing at my mother. A guy who looked to be about nineteen and was high as a kite on something rose on wobbly legs, pointed a handgun in our direction, and tried to fire off a shot.

Luckily, his piece didn't go off. The man stood there for a split second looking stunned, then he turned around and began to run. His junkie ass didn't get far before someone in the crowd fired a shot that hit him in the back. What happened next was vigilante justice at its worst, because the crowd set out after the man and quickly knocked him to the ground.

He disappeared under a frenzied mass of swinging fists and flailing feet, crying out in pain and begging his ghetto jury to have mercy on him. I was right there in the middle of it, too, getting in my licks with everyone else.

Over the din of the mob, I heard my mother's voice scream from somewhere: "Don't kill him, please don't kill him!"

If anything, I began to kick and punch a little harder after hearing that. Then the mob began to bombard the bleeding, delirious deviant with bricks, bottles, and rocks. One person broke from the crowd and bashed a brick upside his head a couple of times, before some Good Samaritan urged everyone to "take it easy before you kill the bastard."

Mama told us later that the man had pulled her into the bushes and attempted to rape her at gunpoint. But first he tried to perform oral sex on her and when he kneeled down to perform that sordid act, he was so high on heroin that he stumbled into the bushes, bringing his location to our attention.

After my mother's assailant awoke from his coma, he eventually pled guilty to sexual assault charges and he was sent away to serve the rest of his sentence, which came to seven to ten years. The first part of his sentence was meted out at Herman Gardens.

He got exactly what he deserved.

The entire experience left my mother badly shaken, to the point where she moved my brothers and me out of Herman Gardens a few weeks later. An older cousin of mine, Addison Hines, managed a public subsidized housing development in nearby Wayne, Michigan. That's how the Hickory Hollow town homes, in Wayne, became my next home.

I definitely didn't want to leave Herman Gardens, because my boys were there, not to mention a lifestyle that I had grown quite comfortable with. But I understood Mama's need to leave after her ordeal.

She had had enough of the Wild West mentality so prevalent at Herman Gardens, but with me it was a case of "you can take the boy out of the ghetto, but you can't take the ghetto out of the boy." I could no more escape my housing project mind-set than I could change the composition of my DNA. I had been so thoroughly programmed to live a certain way that it wouldn't have mattered if we had moved to Beverly Hills.

The town home we moved into was very nice, but it only had two bedrooms, as opposed to the three-bedroom unit we had shared at Herman Gardens. That meant that only Kenny and I made the move with Mama; Steve would have to find a place of his own. Ron had been out of the house for quite some time and was working as an accountant with General Motors.

Wayne is a relatively poor community that was about 95 percent white. It borders another poor town—Inkster, Michigan—that's mostly black and was within walking distance of my new home. I was already familiar with Inkster, because that's where the Seventh-Day Adventist school bus dropped me off at the Peterson Academy.

Living in a predominantly white neighborhood was no big deal to me. I was not in awe or intimidated by whites. As a matter of fact, if anybody was going to be running an intimidation game, it was gonna be me.

I still attended the Peterson Academy after we moved to Wayne. But instead of catching the bus with the other poor kids, I was now dropped off by my mother. That was cool, because the bourgeois black students at Peterson automatically turned their noses up at the ghetto kids who rode the bus to and from school. Plus I had a handful of associates from the old neighborhood at Peterson I hung out with, and who kept me current on what was happening back at Herman Gardens.

I was seeing less and less of my brother Kenny. By this time he had a construction job working as a carpenter's apprentice and was making big money, twenty dollars an hour. His criminal activity tapered off once those big paychecks started coming. If given a chance between making decent money through a legal or illegal means, 99 percent of people will choose the legal route.

One day I went out during recess and got high on reefer with a Peterson schoolmate named Bernard, who today is struggling with a crack addiction. We popped a few Valiums, too, because I was doing pills by that time.

Afterward, we floated back into a church school surrounded by squares and do-gooders who wouldn't have *dreamed* of touching a marijuana joint, much less smoking one on school premises.

Bernard and I returned to our ninth-grade world history classroom, where I sat directly behind him.

"Man, check out our teacher's head," I whispered in a voice that was way too loud. "Is she totin' a gigantic dome, or what?"

Giddy due to our altered state of consciousness, Bernard and I started giggling in class. I really wanted to stop and I honestly tried, but the harder I tried, the funnier the whole deal became. When Bernard tumbled from behind his desk in slow motion and started slowly rolling across the floor guffawing, that was it. I laughed so hard that my sides hurt.

Our grim-faced teacher directed us to the principal's office, where we got another case of the giggles and erupted into belly laughs that rattled the windows. Bernard got suspended because he was suspected of being high, but miraculously I didn't.

But within a month after my family and I moved to Wayne, I finally got kicked out of Peterson for good. I was accused of shooting dice in the bathroom and smoking weed, and I was guilty on both counts. I always had some smoke on me when I went to school and was usually high when I went to class. And I seldom went anywhere without a pair of dice in my pockets.

"You embarrassed me again—I'm through with you!" Mama screamed after I got home and told her what had happened. "I just wish the police would come and get you for good!"

There were rare occasions, however, when Mama actually teased me about my wayward lifestyle. We'd be sitting at the dinner table eating and having a good time when she'd suddenly say, "Gregory, give me a joint! I think I want me one of them joints. How do you do it?"

Then Mama would lean back in her chair and comically curl her lips around an imaginary joint, then glance at me to see if I was taking in how ridiculous she looked. The implication being, *you* look this silly, too.

"Oh, Mama, go on!"

But those lighthearted moments were few and far between. My suspension from Peterson definitely didn't lead to one.

In what had become a familiar mission for Mama, she started gathering information and making phone calls so that I could enroll in a new school.

During a brief period when I was staying home after my suspension, I observed that my new next-door neighbors seemed to be living rather prosperously, because they were buying an awful lot of new stuff.

One day as I watched from the window of my town house, my neighbors brought in a host of Kmart and Sears boxes, then locked their house and drove off a short time later. They hadn't been gone five minutes before I scampered into their backyard, feeling the delicious high that comes from the possibility of making a big scene. It's a rush sweeter than anything cocaine or heroin could ever produce. All my nerve endings were exploding, transmitting information to a brain and muscles that were performing at such a high level that I felt damn near superhuman.

It was a simple matter to kick in the frame on a basement window, which allowed me to quickly slither into the basement and out of sight. I knew the setup of their house was identical to mine, so I raced up the basement stairs and into the kitchen.

I smiled when I got there, because the boxes I had watched my neighbors bring in were sitting empty on the kitchen floor. Their contents were a few yards away in the living room: a new turntable stereo system and a portable color television.

This was the way a home burglary should go—in and out with a minimum of fuss or drama. Why would anyone waste their time at nine-to-five, slaving for pennies a day, when it was possible to do this?

I quickly transported my booty to my house, draping a jacket over both items to hide them from view. I took both pilfered items into my basement and put them into a big storage trunk that Mama rarely opened. Unfortunately, I couldn't get the lid to close all the way once the stereo and television were inside, so I draped a blanket over the trunk.

My stuff should be safe in there until I had a chance to get it out of the house unnoticed, I figured.

A few minutes later I was sitting at the kitchen table, wolfing down a peanut butter and jelly sandwich, when I heard the lady next door screaming at the top of her lungs and weeping as she cursed out the entire neighborhood.

I peeked through the curtain as another neighbor began to console the distraught woman and eased her back into her house to bring an end to the spectacle she was making. Listening to and watching the woman's pain and anguish had no effect on me whatsoever. She should have known better than to flaunt her purchases for the whole neighborhood to see.

Easing the curtain back in place, I went back to eating my sandwich until the wail of a police car's siren split the still afternoon air, then it stopped. I looked out the curtain to see a squad car parked in front of my house. The two cops exited the car and began talking to the two women I had seen a few minutes earlier.

As the cops listened and one of them dutifully took notes, Mama appeared on the scene carrying two bags of groceries. She set them down and listened to the neighbor whose house I had broken into, nodding and periodically patting the woman's back.

At one point Mama glanced in the direction of our house, causing me to scrunch my back against the wall to avoid being detected. Then she picked up her grocery bags and walked with a tired gait toward our house. Letting the curtain ease back into place, I zipped back into the bedroom I shared with Kenny. I quickly kicked off my shoes and lay down on my bed, simultaneously opening a textbook and a school notebook.

As if Mama actually thought I would be studying while suspended from school! She opened the front door and I heard her grumbling, which was a bad sign.

"Hi, Mama. Need help with them bags?" I asked, staying on the bed.

"No, Gregory. Especially since you actually doin' some homework for a change."

"What's wrong? You look mad or somethin'."

Mama sighed. "Somebody broke into the place next door," she grunted. "Broad daylight and nobody seen a thing. Don't make no sense—just as bad as the Gardens."

She began putting away groceries, frowning at the thought that she couldn't outrun the mayhem she'd left Herman Gardens to escape. Frankly, my thoughts weren't on my mother's fears or on anyone else's feelings.

I was lying on the bed trying to figure out how much I could get for the stuff I had just stolen. What I didn't know was that Mama needed something in the basement and had walked down there to get it.

She immediately became suspicious after noticing a blanket draped over her storage trunk. Then Mama saw that the trunk wasn't closed all the way, and an angry, anguished shriek shot up from the basement like a bolt of lightning. What were the fucking odds of me sticking some hot stuff in that trunk and Mama opening it an hour later? Goddamn!

"Greeeeeegory!"

"Yeah, Mama?"

"Get your ass down here right nooooooow!"

Mama was standing there with one hand on her hip, the other on the raised trunk lid. She was glaring at the electronic goods our neighbor claimed had been stolen from her home.

"What is this?"

"What, Mama?"

"Dammit, don't play with me, boy. You 'bout to get hurt! Where did this stereo and television come from? These are the *same* things someone stole from our neighbor's house!"

"I don't know where the stuff came from!" I said, my voice rising. "You think I took that stuff?—I ain't go in that lady's house." I'd racked my brain furiously for an acceptable lie, but given the pressure of the situation and the evidence staring me right in the face, that lame response was the best I could do.

From the expression on Mama's face, you would have thought I just slapped her. She looked numb and zombie-like as she slowly lowered the lid to the trunk, then trudged up the basement stairs. I had never seen her look or act like that, and it alarmed me.

"I been here studying all day, Mama," I shouted upstairs. "Why everything always gotta be my fault?"

My mother was seated at the kitchen table after I walked up the basement stairs. She had both of her thick hands wrapped around her greenish brown Bible and was crying as though she was completely brokenhearted. I was deeply hurt by her obvious agony and stunned that she hadn't whipped me to death.

But I had already denied stealing the merchandise, so I had to stick with my story.

"I done all I can do," Mama said in a tortured voice, barely able to catch her breath between sobs. "God knows I tried to do what I thought was right. But I can't take it no more—I give up."

She paused to gaze up at the kitchen ceiling. Then she said, "You in the Lord's hands now."

Weeping slightly less now, Mama got up from the kitchen table and slowly walked to the wall telephone. She dialed the phone and waited for someone to come on the line, her eyes avoiding me the entire time.

"I want to report a break-in at 1912 Wayne—no, it was my neighbor's house. Uh-uh, I want to report that my son did it. Yes, my son . . . uh-huh, I'm sure. Yes, he's standing right here. Y'all come and get him right now!"

Mama hung up the phone, got up, and shuffled back down the basement stairs without looking in my direction. She took our neighbor's goods out of the trunk, returned them next door, and begged for my neighbor's forgiveness.

Peeking through the curtain, I saw the two of them standing on my neighbor's walkway embracing each other and crying as another cop car rolled to a stop in front of my house. The whole thing had an air of unreality, as if I were trapped in a bad dream that I would wake up from any second.

Mama met with the cops and pointed toward her house. They started trudging up our walkway. I let go of the curtain and sprinted back to my bedroom, where I sat on the bed waiting. I wasn't quite sure for what.

I didn't have to wait long to find out, because Mama was soon standing in the doorway of my bedroom, framed by two white male cops. "There he is," she said in a contemptuous voice, as though talking about a dog turd on the sidewalk. "Take him *outta* here!"

Mama stepped away from the door and the cops walked into my bedroom as if they owned it. The smell of their sweat and the leather of their gunbelts followed them.

"W-w-what?" I stammered. "What's going on?"

One of the cops put a beefy hand under my armpit and lifted me off my bed as if I were a loaf of bread. Neither officer appeared in the mood for denials or heartfelt pleas.

"Put your shoes on so we can go," growled the cop who had lifted me up. "You're under arrest."

"For what?" I screamed at the top of my lungs. "Mama!"

Once I had my shoes on, they roughly shoved my hands behind my back and slapped a pair of cold, heavy metal handcuffs around my wrists. Then I was half pushed, half dragged out of my house. I tried to gaze at my mother on the way out, but she turned her face so she wouldn't have to look at me.

Quite a few of my neighbors were outside to take in the show as I was escorted to the waiting squad car. The credo of the streets demanded that I not display fear or concern, so I made my face a mask of callous indifference. I made eye contact with no one in particular as one of the cops put his hand on my head, roughly pushed me into the backseat of the police car, and closed the door.

One of the cops stayed with me in the car, while the other went to the home of the neighbor I had robbed. "People don't know what kind of fucking trash they're living next door to these days," the officer in the car muttered.

After a few minutes the other cop returned, opened the rear door of the squad car, and jerked me off my seat and out of the police cruiser.

The other cop hopped off the front seat and walked around to where I was standing, looking at his partner quizzically.

"What's the deal?"

"The neighbor doesn't want to press charges," came the disgusted reply. "She got all her stuff back and she feels sorry for the mother." He paused and gave me a murderous look. "Maybe she's scared of this little bastard, too."

The cuffs were removed from my wrists, and it felt damn good to once again have a full range of motion in my arms. Suddenly, one of the cops grabbed my collar.

"But I just know you'll fuck up again, and next time I don't give a damn if we got charges against you or not," he said, blowing his stinking breath in my face. "We'll take care of your little ass. Now get the hell off the streets, punk!"

He pushed me hard in the back and I stumbled before catching my balance. Aware that every eye was on me, I straightened up and did a mac daddy pimp walk back to my front door.

Mama was seated at the kitchen table with her back to me when I went back inside. I cleared my throat, about to reach deep into my apology bag, but she wasn't hearing any of it.

"Just get on outta my face," she snapped, red hot with humiliation. "Unnerstand, though, that every time I catch you doing something wrong I'm callin' the cops on you. I'm gonna let the authorities handle you, 'cause I can't. Plus, when you finished with high school, I want you outta here!"

Without another word, I went back to my room and plopped down on my bed. How in the world could my own mother have called the police on me? As I pondered that mystery, I heard some words from the kitchen that chilled me to the core and that I have never forgotten.

"Why, Lord, why? What have I done wrong?"

That comment hit me like an electric shock. I couldn't get it out of my head for several days.

Throughout the trials and tribulations of our relationship, Mama's devotion to the Seventh-Day Adventist Church never wavered. Nor did her insistence on dragging me to church each and every weekend. Now that we were in Wayne, Mama was attending a Seventh-Day Adventist church located in Inkster, instead of worshiping with the congregation I had grown up with in Detroit. The church location may have been different, but the same old tedious, boring routine was firmly in place. My solution was to twist up some killer weed before going to church. Then I would sit in church and trip hard on all the sanctimonious Holy Rollers.

VI

"GET THAT SCUM OUTTA HERE!"

Now that my family and I were residents of Wayne, Michigan, Mama decided to enroll me in Wayne Memorial High School. Talk about culture shock!

I had gone from a school that was private, all black, and mostly full of middle-class achievers, to one that was public, just about all white, and filled with kids from the lower rungs of the socioeconomic ladder. I'd clearly shot myself in the foot by getting thrown out of Peterson, but I wasn't about to let on.

It was hardly as though I had any options when it came to getting an education, because Mama had already made it clear that the minute I stopped attending school, I had to move out.

My first day at Wayne High I came bopping through the front door like I owned the joint, with my long Super Fly perm flowing out from beneath my Borsalino hat and my sharp three-piece suit and alligator kicks making an unmistakable statement.

Which was: "I am every inch a Detroit street tough, so all you punks and wimps need to understand there's a new sheriff in town." The word was already out that I was from the city, so I was given a pretty wide berth from Day One.

I had a crazed look in my eyes, a perpetual scowl on my face, and packed a pistol that I kept tucked in its familiar hiding place, my waistband. If anyone dared to gaze in my direction, they were greeted with, "Whatchoo lookin' at, bitch? I'll put your punk ass in the hospital!"

Being forced to attend Wayne enraged me, and I made damn sure that everybody from the principal on down realized it. No one went out of their way to befriend me, which was fine, too.

After taking about a week to scope out my new surroundings, I recruited a couple of wannabe thugs who were hungry and had a little heart. They served as my eyes and ears around the school, because I needed someone to watch my back. Then I set out to let the student body understand just who the fuck they were dealing with.

Like a famished shark zeroing in on straggling minnows, I accosted students in the hallway, the gymnasium, the playground—it didn't matter.

My exotic inner-city clothing and mannerisms, as well as my predatory scowl, had most of them scared shitless before I even uttered a word. "You best have me some muthafuckin' money *every* day," I'd murmur in my best Jimmy Cagney voice. "Else I'll stomp yo' bitch ass right in front of yo' lil' pussy friends."

My victims were usually catatonic by then, but to make sure we were on the same wavelength, sometimes I'd put my hand around their necks and squeeze.

Occasionally the malice and rage I showed were an act, but not always. As a youth I was angry a lot of the time, partially because of my perception of white people and what they were doing to minorities in this country. However, the rest of my rage was coming from a wellspring I didn't quite comprehend. During much of my childhood, I was mad at the world.

Wayne High had a few "burnout" students, white guys who got high all the time and who sold drugs. They thought they were tough and challenged me during my first days in school. To put them in their place, I'd let them get a glimpse of my gun tucked into my waistband, then I'd have some of my Herman Gardens crew come to the school in a show of force.

I had no problems after that. I had the burnouts so well trained that they reflexively handed over their weed and pills when they saw me coming. Then I'd turn around and sell the same shit to the customers the burnouts had cultivated before I came to Wayne High. Definitely a sweet setup!

I felt the school was wide-open terrain for me to do as I damn well pleased, because everyone was so much weaker than I was. Once you've been battle tested by the streets of inner-city Detroit, not much can compare.

One time I fell asleep in class and my pistol fell out of my pants and clattered to the floor. I bent down to pick it up and caught two white guys staring at me in wide-eyed amazement. "Y'all mutha-fuckas didn't see *shit*!" I whispered menacingly out of the corner of my mouth. That was all the convincing they needed.

As had been the case at Peterson, I became Wayne High's chief shakedown artist and locker burglar, bar none. And just like at Peterson, I amazed students and teachers alike by performing at a high academic level.

Maybe that last factor was why Wayne High's assistant principal, Mr. Stratton, took a special interest in me. I've got to hand it to him, he was pretty slick in the way he went about establishing a relationship with me.

I was in class one day when the teacher told me Mr. Stratton wanted to see me.

"Why? What did I do?"

"Gregory, he didn't say," came the exasperated reply. "But he wants to see you right after class."

I swaggered down the middle of the hall after class, parting students like Moses parting the Red Sea. Knowing better than to look at me, they all averted their eyes and suddenly found themselves intrigued by the contents of their locker.

I hadn't been sitting in the office a hot minute before Mr. Stratton had me ushered into his little cubbyhole.

"So, how are you finding your experience at Wayne thus far?" he said, smiling as he shook my hand.

"It's okay," I answered, wondering why Mr. Stratton wasn't cutting to the chase. I didn't have time to mess around with him right before lunch, because this was the best time of day to shake down students for money.

"You know, Greg," Mr. Stratton said, gesturing for me to have a seat in front of his desk, "you are without question one of the strongest personalities and leaders at Wayne Memorial High."

Peering back at Wayne's assistant principal through hooded eyes, I wondered if he really meant to say that he knew I was jacking everybody up and selling drugs.

"Greg, I want you to do me a favor," he said, something no assistant principal had ever uttered to me. I couldn't wait to hear his request.

"If you don't mind, I want you to keep an eye on my school for me," Mr. Stratton said, coupling his words with an admiring smile. "To be honest, we're having problems with some of the students here. We could fight a lot of the negative peer pressure around here if students like you would help me out."

I nodded incredulously, not sure if I believed what I was hearing.

"I want you to use your leadership skills to keep things calm and under control for me, Greg. Think you can do that for me?"

"Sure, Mr. Stratton. No problem."

I came out of his office with a serious glide in my stride, laughing that I had not only cowed all of Wayne's students, but now had the frickin' assistant principal sanctioning my strong-arm tactics. Further confirming what I already knew beyond a doubt—I was the motherfucking man!

It was business as usual for me after that—a shakedown here, a drug sale there.

Unbelievably, my regime was brought to an end by a little punk whose lunch money I used to lift on a regular basis. One day he tried to get out of making his payment to me and, snarling, I pulled my gun and waved it in his face. My magic charm worked as it had countless times before, so I strolled away from our encounter thinking nothing more of it.

That afternoon after lunch as I was retrieving some things from my locker, Mr. Stratton came up behind me.

"Greg, could we talk a moment?" he said, causing me to whirl around to block his view of my locker's contents.

"Yeah, what's up? What's goin' on, Mr. Stratton?"

"I'd really rather talk in my office. Confidentially." My antennae went up immediately. Could this be about that wimp I shook down earlier in the day? Naw, because he wouldn't talk—I had him trained too well to do that.

But I would still need to ditch my pistol, which was poking me in the small of my back as I stood talking to Mr. Stratton.

"All right then, Mr. Stratton. Gotta use the bathroom first."

"Me too, Greg. I'll head into the can with you and make a pit stop."

Students came streaming out of the bathroom the minute Mr. Stratton and I showed up, leaving burning cigarettes sitting on sinks and on the windowsill.

I had a hard time pissing with Mr. Stratton standing at the urinal right beside mine. Naturally I didn't have to go to the bathroom—I had to ditch my gun, and fast! Calm down, I told myself. If he really just wants to talk, you will have thrown away a perfectly good piece for nothing.

So I eked out a few drops of urine, washed my hands, and followed Mr. Stratton to his office. While his back was to me, I did push my gun down into my pants a little more securely than normal. And I chided myself for not going into a bathroom stall where I would have had some privacy.

As soon as he closed his office door behind me, Mr. Stratton's friendly, I'm-your-pal demeanor vanished. His tone became brusque and businesslike, and his eyes narrowed as he began to talk to me.

"Sit down, Greg," he commanded. "So, is everything okay with you?" He shot me a sneaky, I've-got-you-pegged look.

"Yeah man, I'm straight. What's up?"

"There's a rumor going around school that you've been selling drugs."

"Man, I ain't sellin' no damn drugs! You seen my grades."

Mr. Stratton walked around his desk and gripped the arms of the wooden chair I was seated in. He bent down, putting the two of us nearly nose-to-nose.

"Look, Greg, if you're selling drugs, just tell me and we can work something out. But don't lie to me."

"Hey man, I tole you I ain't sellin' no drugs. Why would I come up here and do something stupid like that?"

Mr. Stratton straightened up and took a couple of steps toward the window in his office. I used that opportunity to slide a plastic baggie full of pills out of my sock and into the bottom of my seat cushion. Mr. Stratton whirled around and caught me with my back half turned to him.

He rushed toward me with an accusatory look on his face. "What's that bulge behind you, Greg? You're not carrying a gun, are you?" With that he reached down to touch the mysterious protrusion on my back, and I immediately popped out of my chair and pushed him away.

"Yo, man, don't be touchin' me," I yelled. "First you accuse me of sellin' drugs, now you trying to say I'm packin'. I don't have to put up with this shit—I'm outta here."

I opened the door to Mr. Stratton's office in time to see two uniformed cops come striding into the outer office.

"He's got a gun, he's got a gun!" Mr. Stratton shouted.

The cops were on me instantly, wrestling me roughly to the ground, pushing my face against the dirty floor. I didn't try to resist as one of them yanked my pistol from my waistband, then handcuffed my arms behind my back.

"You got any other weapons?"

"Naw, I ain't got nothin', man."

One of the cops had his service revolver drawn as they pulled me to my feet and escorted me out of the office area.

"Get that scum outta here," Mr. Stratton yelled. "For good."

Those cops pushed me every step of the way down the long hallway leading to the front door, which was unnecessary. As they did so, all the wimpy white kids that I humiliated were actually lined up in the hallway and clapping and applauding as I was hustled out of Wayne Memorial High School.

I tried to catalog as many of their faces as I could when I was leaving, because I was planning on having the last laugh. And when I did, we'd see who'd grin and cheer then. Muthafuckas!

Once the cops put me in their car, they drove me to downtown Detroit, to the Wayne County Jail. A police photographer had me hold up one of those little black felt boards with my name spelled on it in white letters.

This huge flash went off twice to get a frontal and side picture of me. I could feel the heat coming off that camera, and it left purplish dots floating in my vision for about two minutes.

Then they made me rub my fingers through this black ink that was used to fingerprint me. I was given a tube of white cream to clean my fingers, with a coarse brown paper towel like you find in public rest rooms.

I was allowed to make one phone call, and I made the mistake of placing it to Mama.

"Collect call from Gregory Mathis. Will you accept?"

"No!"

"But tell her I'm in jail, operator!"

"I know exactly where he is," Mama said quietly. Click!

The phone was taken from me, and I was directed to a jail holding area containing honest-to-God adult thugs, not little seventeen-year-old toy gangsters like me. I instinctively went into character—hard, scowling, and thoroughly unfazed by everything I saw. Just behind the public mask, though, I was freaking out.

After walking down a cool corridor while I felt the gaze of every inmate in the place on me, I was directed into a two-man cell inhabited by an Evander Holyfield look-alike. He was stripped down to his drawers, the better to display the kind of rippling muscles usually seen on boxers and wrestlers. He smelled like he needed to wash his ass, too.

"I'm sleeping on top," he said in a booming voice as he stood beside our bunk bed. Frankly, as long as he wasn't climbing on top of me I didn't give a fuck where he slept. Sleep wasn't something I got much of that night, anyway. I lay in my bunk listening to the random grunts and coughs and snores of the other inmates as I replayed the day's events in my head.

Why had Mama hung the phone up on me at a time when I needed her more than ever? I wasn't angry with her, though, because on some level I understood that she did what she had to do. And even though I was lonely and scared in my jail cell, I knew that Mama had my best interests at heart.

When morning dawned, a deputy appeared at my cell with a tray holding two cartons of milk and two paper bowls filled with breakfast cereal. As I hopped off my bunk to get my cereal, my monstrous cellmate walked back from the bars of our cell carrying both of our breakfasts.

"What up, man?" I said in my best tough guy voice.

"Whatchoo mean, what up, youngblood?" he said, placing his hulking body directly in front of me. He was about three inches taller than I was and easily had me by one hundred pounds.

"You ain't paid enough dues in here to be gettin' no breakfast," he said, seeming amused. "Don't you see how big I am, boy? I need both of these breakfasts to fill up. Got a problem with that?"

I made a snap assessment: If I swung on him, they wouldn't find enough of me to cart to the jail infirmary.

"Naw, g'wan ahead, man. Ain't no thang. I don't eat cereal no way." Actually I did eat cereal, and I was starving. I sat on the bottom bunk trying not to listen as my cellmate slurped down my cereal.

I had come face-to-face with a tough guy who was the real deal, and it looked like my best bet was to make another call to my mother. Evander Holyfield's look-alike was released not too long after breakfast was served, to my relief. As soon as he left, I decided that no one else was going to make me back down while I was in jail.

The deputies let the prisoners out for some exercise and recreation time, allowing me to clean up in a poker game. Instead of money we played for snacks and smokes, so I took my winnings and hid them under my pillow. However, when I put my hand under my pillow later that day, I felt nothing.

"WHO THE FUCK BEAT ME FOR MY SNACKS AND SQUARES?" I bellowed like I was out of my damn mind. "Which muthafucka did it?"

A hard-core, old head inmate immediately hopped to his feet and grabbed me in my collar. "I took 'em, little motherfuck! Now what you gonna do—whup me or something?"

I took my knee and rammed his balls so hard that I'm surprised they didn't touch his tonsils. While he was bent over, moaning in agony, I pushed my antagonist to the floor and grabbed a broom with a thick wooden handle. I broke the broom on one of the jail cells, then I commenced to kicking that inmate's ass with the handle.

I beat that sucka until the guards came and dragged me off to an isolation cell. Good thing, too, because I was so fired up—so angry and scared—that I felt like I could kill. That's a scary feeling when the heat of the moment is gone.

Still, I was pleased with myself because I had sent an unmistakable message—that I wasn't some little punk to be trifled with.

When I returned from solitary, I didn't have any more problems with prisoners trying to intimidate me.

One day not too long after I had gone to jail, one of the guards told me that I had a visitor. When I went into the visiting room and saw Mama in there, a big ol' grin automatically spread across my face. I knew Moms would eventually thaw out and come see her baby boy.

But when I got closer and saw the worried expression on my mother's haggard face, my grin froze.

"Hi baby," she said, sitting on the other side of a wall made of cinderblock and glass and talking to me through a telephone.

"Hey, Mama. Why you lookin' so sad? Don't worry about me, because I'm fine here. I'm straight."

"I know you're gonna be fine," Mama said, which made me feel better. "You're a tough kid, Greg. It's not you, it's . . ." My mother's lips began to tremble and she was unable to continue.

"What's wrong, Ma?" I blurted. "Is something wrong with Kenny? Is it Ron or Steve? What, Mama?"

"No, Greg, thank God it's not them. It's me, Gregory. . . ." That threw me for a loop, just like the night when Mama was accosted at Herman Gardens. Nothing was supposed to happen to Mama.

"You?"

"Uh-huh. I had this blood in my stool. . . ."

"Blood?"

"Yes. I went to the doctors and they . . . they say I got cancer." I rose halfway out of my chair, my eyes burning into Mama's.

"Cancer, Mama?" Everything she said after that, including "operation" and "malignant" and "exploratory surgery" was lost in a whirlwind of emotions. Only one word made a distinct impression. Cancer.

"They probably made a mistake, Ma," I said. "You know them doctors don't always know what they talkin' about."

"Now, Greg, it might be benign," Mama said, finally unable to stop the tears from falling. "There might not be a problem at all." Mama paused for a moment to dab at her eyes. "Lord, Lord, Lord, please help me."

The moment she said that, I couldn't hold the tears back any longer. "Mama, I know I've been messin' up and makin' things hard for you," I said, blubbering in the visiting room of the Wayne County Jail. "But I'm gonna change up, Ma, I swear I am. You'll see."

My mother looked at me with a wan smile. "Greg, don't swear unless you mean it," she said.

"I mean it, Ma—square business. I'm gonna do it for you, Ma. You'll see."

Mama gave me a hard look, trying to see if I was sincere or not.

"Greg, you ain't never been a bad person," she said. "You get into trouble, but you're not an evil boy. I believe you can change, I really do. But don't do it for me, son. Do it for yourself. I done lived my life, Gregory, but yours is still ahead of you."

She gestured at the drab green walls of the jail visiting room and at the glass partition separating us. "This what you want from your life, son?"

I shook my head and put my hand against the glass. Mama put her palm against the glass opposite mine.

"I swear I'll change, Mama," I said, feeling another wave of sobs coming. "You'll see. You'll see."

Mama gave me a little smile, and we continued to talk for a few minutes more, although for the life of me I have no idea what about. Because my mind was really on one thing, and that was the cancer I was praying wasn't inside her body.

A guard finally walked over and mercifully brought that painful visit to an end. I stood in the visiting room watching Mama leave, then I walked slack-jawed back to my cell, in the throes of the lowest moment of my life.

Mama has cancer! I should be there for her during her time of crisis, just like she's always been there for me. Instead, here I am in jail—giving her something else to worry her poor mind.

Metal jail bars slowly glided past on my left and my right as I trudged back to my cell, escorted by a guard. I was so numb that the scenes inside the jail passed before my eyes like a silent movie, without the usual hum of the ventilation system, inmates yelling and playing music in the recreation yard, and jail employees passing messages over the intercom system.

Mama has cancer!

When I finally reached my cell, an old convict who had taken the place of the huge guy was inside our cell. Jailed on fraud charges, he rarely went out to the recreation yard to pump iron or play basketball. He pretty much just ate and slept as he awaited his trial.

"What's the matter, youngblood?" he asked after I sat on my bunk for several minutes with my mouth gaping open.

"My mama's sick, man," I mumbled, not even turning to look at my cellmate. "She got cancer, and I gotta help her. I gotta get out of here."

Then I lowered my head into my hands, hoping the old con would take the hint and leave me the hell alone.

"Best thing you can do is change up, youngblood, turn your life around," he said quietly. "Look like you got a good head on your shoulders. Don't throw your life in the trash can like I done."

I glanced up and the old con was staring at me with a benevolent look that touched my soul. I shuddered and looked away, wondering if he was one of those messengers from God Mama was always talking about. Then I lay back on my bunk without saying a word.

God, I have not always done the right thing, I prayed silently. But if you let Mama get well, I swear I will turn my life around. I swear that, God.

Mama underwent surgery about a week later and our worst fears were confirmed—she did have colon cancer. I went to God again with another promise to turn my life around and turn my back on crime in exchange for my mother's life.

When my case went to court, my court-appointed attorney and I stood before Judge Kaufman in Wayne County Circuit Court. My lawyer and I had agreed that I would be willing to plead guilty to a misdemeanor charge of a firearms violation, if the court would agree to dismiss the concealed weapon charge, which was a felony.

"So, you're pleading guilty to the misdemeanor?" Judge Kaufman asked, looking me over closely. "How old are you and what grade are you in?"

I cleared my throat, then took a deep breath. "I'm seventeen, your honor, and I'm in the eleventh grade."

"Okay, then. I've talked to your mother, who is ill and couldn't be here in court today. But she's an exceptional woman. I have also contacted Wayne Memorial High School, which wants nothing more to do with you, and have discovered that your aptitude tests are exceptionally high."

Judge Kaufman studied a pile of papers on his desk, prior to giving me the best break I had ever received in my life. "Mr. Mathis," he said slowly, "if in six months you do not have a high school diploma or a GED, you will go to jail. I will leave it entirely up to you. Do you understand?"

I gladly took that deal, which overjoyed Mama when she learned of it. I wasted little time enrolling in an adult-education GED program. Judge Kaufman's decree that I finish my high school education or return to jail turned out to be a triple blessing. The first came in the form of Annette Rainwater, a dynamic, earthy black woman who was a political activist in Detroit and was serving as an adviser to Reverend Jesse Jackson's Operation Push—a program for the empowerment of African Americans, which includes youth motivation and scholarships.

I met her because she happened to address my GED class one day. They say God moves in mysterious ways, and my introduction to Rainwater would pay dividends years later in ways I couldn't begin to appreciate as a seventeen-year-old.

The second blessing was that the GED course introduced me to *The Autobiography of Malcolm X*, the most profoundly moving book I have ever read in my life. I had an eerie feeling that the book was written just for me, because so much of what Malcolm experienced could easily have been overlaid on my life up to that point.

The third blessing came in the form of a mesmerizing civil rights activist that I had never heard of prior to the summer of 1977, a gentleman named the Reverend Jesse Jackson. He came to speak at a citywide school forum I attended at Cobo Hall Auditorium, the same place where I had robbed concertgoers as a gang member months earlier.

The best way to describe it was that Jackson had an electric aura that filled Cobo Hall. Many of the women in the arena acted as though they were having trouble breathing when Jackson began speaking to us.

"You as young black men and women are doing the thing that your enemies dread the most," he said in a singsong delivery that rose and fell hypnotically. "You are putting books in your hands and knowledge in your heads. If you were putting guns in your hands and dope in your heads, your enemies would rejoice."

Jackson paused and looked directly at the front row, where I happened to be seated. "If you were dealing with guns and dope, it would only be a matter of time before those who want to see you fall would own you. Failing at that, they'd have justification to incarcerate or *kill* you."

I listened wide-eyed, amazed at the degree to which Jackson's words and Malcolm X's converged and made perfect sense. "But you are taking the first steps to avoiding the traps of the ghetto. Because one thing your enemies will *never* be able to do, no matter how hard they try, is make nobodies out of somebodies.

"As long as you can be made to think that you're a nobody, your enemies will have you believing that nothing good can *ever* come from you. Or anybody that looks like you, for that matter.

"Well, let me tell you right now, young people, that you *are somebody!*" I looked in awe at this man who had a bunch of blasé, cynical young inner-city adults buzzing and rocking in their seats as if they were at a Baptist revival meeting. It marked the first time I had seen anyone with such a prodigious gift for communication and leadership.

"Say it with me!" Jackson said in a rich voice that filled every square inch of Cobo Hall, "I aaaam somebody. I aaaam somebody."

When the forum was over, I waited until the other students had finished swarming Jackson, acting like groupies fussing over the Jackson 5 or the Beatles. I wanted to have a serious conversation with this inspirational man, not fuss over him.

Just as he was about to step toward the door, I intercepted him and blocked his path.

"Mr. Jackson," I said as he reached down to shake my hand, "you really inspired me. I think I may be one of those leaders of tomorrow that you talked about. I want to help steer brothers around some of those traps you talked about."

"Uh-huh," he said. "Your heart is in the right place, but to win young peoples' minds and souls, you've got to have ammunition. A GED only allows you to go to boot camp. You need to go to college to get the kind of ammunition you need. You've got to prepare yourself before you can properly lead others. Understand?"

I nodded enthusiastically as Jackson dug into his wallet and pulled out a business card. I noticed how huge his hands were as he took the card and gently laid it in the palm of my hand.

"A year from now, I want to hear what you've done to improve yourself, to prepare yourself. We got a deal?" He gestured to Annette. "Rainwater—work with this young man!"

"We've got a deal," I responded, grinning happily, ecstatic that he'd taken the time to talk to me one on one. That moment with him marked the first time in my life I'd ever considered attending college.

Along with earning a GED, another condition of my probation required me to be employed that summer. When I told that to a friend of mine, Lela Tennile, she suggested that I apply to the McDonald's fast-food restaurant where she worked in the evenings.

McDonald's! The last thing I wanted to do was wear one of their corny uniforms, standing around flipping burgers all day. But I didn't want to hurt her feelings, so I suggested that I look at some other options first.

Sheeeit, I couldn't be seen in no damn McDonald's! I would lose my rep forever if word got out that I was working there. So I took a couple of other odd jobs. One was in a Wayne gas station, where I pumped gas, wiped windshields, and checked motor oil.

"Check your tire pressure, sir. Yessir!"

One day I was cleaning the windshield of a white couple when the gas station owner came walking over to me with his hands on his hips.

"You didn't wipe that properly," he said, frowning as he pointed to a faint insect smear. "Do the whole thing over again!"

Without thinking I yielded to my first impulse, which was to get blazing mad and shoot off at the mouth.

"Who you think you're talking to?" I roared, slamming down the squeegee I had been holding. "You don't talk to me like that, 'cause I'll kick your muthafuckin' ass! In fact, why don't you take this fucking job and shove it!"

My next job was at a car wash in Wayne. I lasted about a week there, because it was too damn much work for too little pay. Not only was I tired as hell from constantly drying cars from eight in the morning until six in the evening, but that gig was hurting my image as well. I was so fatigued afterward that I was falling asleep in my afternoon GED classes.

So I quit that job, too. However, I couldn't stay unemployed for long, because unemployment equaled jail time. And I had no intention of going back there.

My brother Kenny had been in the army for about a year and seemed to be doing okay for himself. He was getting three squares a day, traveling, and making some money, too, so I decided to look Uncle Sam's way.

When I told Mama about that plan, she was all for it. Having seen that Kenny hadn't been shipped off to some foreign hot spot and appeared to be prospering, she had given her trust to the military.

Six weeks after my release from prison I went to an army recruiting office on Grand River Street in Detroit. Patriotism was not my motivation. More than anything, I needed something that would keep me out of trouble and put some money in my pocket. Military service was something that quite a few black men from the inner city and from my neighborhood turned to during that era.

I encountered an engaging black sergeant whose starched uniform was festooned with ribbons and medals. I had no idea what they represented, but I was impressed by the way that sergeant carried himself, as if he were General Douglas MacArthur. He gave me this great pitch about all the wonderful training the army could give me.

I could earn money for college, and the army would actually make it possible for me to buy a home after I left the service. The more he talked, the more pumped I became about joining the army.

There was a lot of paperwork to fill out, and I hit a snag when I encountered the section asking whether I had a criminal record. I asked the sergeant if my juvenile record would pose a problem and he replied he wasn't sure but would look into it.

A few days later he called me back and said my induction paperwork had been declined. I assumed it was because of my criminal record. The rejection was a slap at my ego and left me feeling down and dejected.

When that fell through, I reluctantly trudged to the McDonald's where Lela worked. It was located in Romulus, Michigan, a suburb that adjoins Wayne. I walked into the McDonald's, which was across the street from Romulus High School, and filled out a job application.

I was half hoping that McDonald's would reject me just like the Army had. But as has often been the case in my life, God had something else in mind.

I wasn't exactly overjoyed to learn that I had been approved for employment, allowing me to join forces with Ronald McDonald as opposed to Uncle Sam. Like Sam would have, Ronald demanded that I cut my luxuriant Jeri curl or put it into a net.

The manager of the restaurant was a mild-mannered white guy named Dale. He was a decent individual and very encouraging. Dale was a natural teacher and was always willing to show me the ropes when it came to running the McDonald's franchise he managed.

When I first started I had to be there at 6:30 in the morning, which was when the opening shift reported for work. One of my first tasks was to clear the parking lot of the beer cans, bottles, and other trash that had been tossed there overnight.

Then I had to clean the grease trap and load the restaurant's freezer before going to work on the grill. Furthermore, throughout the morning and afternoon I had to go outside periodically and pick up trash.

I distinctly remember making sure that I never went outside when school buses were across the street, because my ego couldn't withstand having an audience watch me pick up litter.

Believe it or not, I actually had a sense of purpose the entire time I worked at that McDonald's in Romulus, Michigan. That's because during orientation I was told that I could become the manager or otherwise move up the corporate hierarchy.

Being able to wrap my arms around a concrete goal brought a sense of direction to my life.

After years of living hand-to-mouth and hustling, I was starting to achieve a degree of financial security, which was a strange feeling. Stranger still, it was due to what I had long considered the most dead-end of jobs!

Another windfall suddenly materialized, in the form of a $350 Social Security check that I began to receive every month. I got it because my father was disabled, I think from diabetes. Whatever the reason, I wasn't about to look a gift horse in the mouth.

I used the Social Security money to buy a green Ford Grand Torino that was three years old.

With reliable transportation at my disposal, I was always on time for the opening shift at McDonald's. Dale, the manager, quickly noticed that I was very responsible and very inquisitive.

People working the grill typically didn't ask him the kinds of questions I posed. When confronted with one of my queries, Dale was very deliberate and very patient in giving an explanation. Often he would stop whatever task he was engaged in at the moment and explain the underlying business rationale. And he occasionally gave me a shot at duties such as taking inventory. Even though that was something managers were responsible for, Dale found me to be a quick study.

Being assigned to the grill was a fortunate assignment, because I wouldn't have lasted a day working with some of the rude folks who walked up to the front counter. That definitely would not have been a good fit, given my nasty temper.

So being tucked away on the grill was fine with me and I gave Mickey Dee's 101 percent. Mama and Lela both were delighted I was demonstrating a commitment to succeed through legal means.

Of course word got around to my boys that I was gigging at McDonald's, and they dropped by to clown on me from time to time. Some of their barbs and jokes stung, but I never let on. Everybody I'd known from the streets was starting to wind up in prison, addicted to narcotics, or dead. Given those alternatives, being one of Ronald McDonald's didn't seem too bad.

"Go ahead and laugh," I told my friends, "because one day I'm gonna wind up owning a McDonald's franchise." That declaration only made my boys laugh even harder and redoubled my determination to succeed.

VII

EASTERN MICHIGAN UNIVERSITY

After I had been at McDonald's for four months, I confronted Dale. I needed to discuss something that had been weighing on my mind.

"Dale, I want to be an assistant manager," I said, watching his expression carefully. "And I want to go to college."

The little smile Dale gave told me that he wasn't surprised. "Yeah, I think we can work that out," he said simply.

Once you let on that you have ambition, you seem to encounter two kinds of people. The first are helpers, like Dale, who do everything they can to help make your dream a reality.

People like him are in the minority, unfortunately, because far too many people want to rain on your parade and enjoy watching you fall short of your objective. That last description fit another young black male who was working at the same McDonald's and who was jealous of my increasing responsibility.

He allowed his pettiness to surface by picking on Lela, who he knew was my friend. Second, he bad-mouthed me to other restaurant employees by telling them about my criminal background. I was trying really hard to keep the street thug in me submerged, but that asshole plucked on my last nerve.

Things eventually came to a head and the two of us got into a shoving match inside the restaurant. I was devastated and disgusted with myself afterward, figuring that all my planning, hard work, and dedication had been ruined by my impulsiveness.

Feeling uncharacteristically nervous, I approached Dale with my side of the story. Then Dale weighed the evidence my antagonist offered. After sifting through our conflicting stories, to my relief Dale fired that punk.

I wound up staying at the Romulus store for a year and was promoted to assistant manager. I initially was a business administration major in college due to McDonald's. I felt that a degree in that area would help me advance within the corporation.

As an assistant manager, I was responsible for supervising staff, making sure the cash register receipts added up correctly, and watching over the restaurant's inventory. Even though the employees in the franchise where I worked were 70 percent white, I had no problem supervising them.

I had a flexible management style that changed based on the personality or demeanor of whomever I happened to be supervising. I saw that I had a talent for making people feel that I understood and identified with them, which was gratifying, because I intuitively understood that it was hard to advance in management without people skills.

I may be one of those rare individuals who can say that toiling at Mickey Dee's represented a significant turning point in my life. My stint there was the first time I had ever put all my focus and energy into making money in a totally legal way.

However, it still didn't address my goal of attending college.

As he had on many occasions in the past, my older cousin, Addison Hines, came to the rescue. Mama suggested that I talk to Addison and my oldest brother, Ron, since they had both attended college.

Whenever you ask Addison for a helping hand, he never checks his calendar, rolls his eyes, or says "Lemme get back to you." He simply rolls up his sleeves and takes care of business. He did it when it came to getting Mama into a new housing development in Wayne, and he came through like a champ when it came to my college objective.

After checking around, Addison found out that his alma mater, Eastern Michigan University, had an affirmative action program that admitted students with GEDs on a trial basis.

The moment he told me that marked one of the few instances I've been the victim of an inferiority complex. The program sounded tantalizing, but I seriously questioned whether I could get into Eastern Michigan, which is located in Ypsilanti, Michigan, about sixty miles west of Detroit. College was for rich kids, not ghetto rats like me.

But my mouth had backed me into a corner. Addison further complicated things by suggesting that we visit Eastern Michigan's campus.

"Uh, what about my criminal record?" I asked hesitantly as we sat at the kitchen table in my mother's townhouse.

"Well, if they ask if you have any adult convictions, you answer no," Addison answered reassuringly. "You were convicted as a juvenile, not an adult."

"But how am I going to pay for this?"

"You're working at McDonald's, and you can get student loans," Addison responded, not relenting an inch. "Just work your way through college like a lot of other people have."

So in July 1978 Addison and I hopped into his Oldsmobile Cutlass and headed to Eastern Michigan University. Mama was just glowing when we left, which made me feel like a million dollars. Instead of the fly clothing I typically favored, I opted for a conservative shirt with a button-down collar, a tie, slacks, and blazer.

Addison made encouraging small talk as we rode west along Interstate 94 headed toward Eastern Michigan. Two years ago, I wouldn't have listened to much he had to say. But as we traveled toward the first college campus I'd ever set foot on, I hung on his every word.

He had graduated from Eastern Michigan with a degree in education, then went on to earn a master's in guidance and counseling. So he knew what the hell he was talking about.

"One thing you'll find about college," he said, talking as if I had already been admitted, "is there's lots of freedom, lots of women, and lots of parties."

He gazed from the road briefly and looked over at me in the passenger seat. "I know you like to party, but don't let that mess you up. Eastern Michigan is the party university of the state, okay?"

I nodded, intrigued by the thought of lots of parties, lots of women, and the freedom to explore both. Yeah!

"You're going to be working, too, so you're not going to have a lot of time for outside stuff," Addison continued. "Discipline yourself—define the hours you're going to study and do it."

I nodded again, this time in agreement. I coveted college so much that I could taste it.

When Addison's Cutlass pulled onto the campus of Eastern Michigan University, I gawked out the window in amazement. The school looked like a town out of a Norman Rockwell painting, with picturesque, rolling greens hills, huge trees, and young white and black people milling about as if they didn't have a care in the world.

None of them wore the hard, desperate expressions I had grown so accustomed to at Herman Gardens.

I felt a sudden urge to laugh, then a desire to turn around and drive home, so I wouldn't waste my time or Addison's. But I said nothing.

We parked our car and went directly to Eastern Michigan's administration building, where Addison had set up an appointment with the person in charge of minority appointments. Clarence Lyte was a brother in his mid-thirties who was short, dark-skinned, and had a down-to-earth, reassuring way of dealing with people.

I immediately sensed that he was sincere about helping me and wasn't some Uncle Tom gatekeeper. After giving me a firm handshake when we entered his impressive office, which had a big bookcase and plaques and diplomas on the walls, Mr. Lyte directed me to have a seat.

There was a brief moment of silence before Addison took charge of the conversation.

"The reason I brought Greg in here, Clarence, is because he's a very smart young man. He's completing his GED and wants to get a college education to realize his full potential." Addison continued to talk as Mr. Lyte listened attentively. I was dying to get a word in myself, because I wanted to sell myself, instead of having Addison do all the heavy lifting.

During a lapse in the conversation, I finally dived in headfirst. "Mr. Lyte, if you let me in here, I think you'll see that I'll turn out to be one of your best students," I began, speaking in a confident, steady voice. "I want to major in business administration, then become one of the top executives at the McDonald's Corporation."

Mr. Lyte nodded his head approvingly. "Sounds like you got your future all mapped out," he said. "A lot of the students here don't have a clue what they want to do until their third or fourth year of school.

"I admire your drive and direction, but you may want to get a good sense of where your skill levels are before you pick a major." He followed that up by giving me an application to fill out.

Addison and I jabbered away excitedly during the drive back to Detroit. We had convinced ourselves that I was in, otherwise Mr. Lyte wouldn't have spoken to me the way he did.

I was so hyped, I completed Eastern Michigan's application the same day I brought it home.

After that, there was nothing to do but wait, which isn't something I excel at. For three weeks, I asked Mama if anything had come in the mail from Eastern Michigan. And every time, the answer was, "No, Greg. But good things come to those who wait." That may be true in a biblical sense perhaps, but I had only applied to one college and was growing increasingly impatient and anxious waiting for that school to respond.

Eventually, I began calling Eastern Michigan every day to check on the status of my application. In August, about two weeks before classes were scheduled to start, I finally got what I had been looking and praying for—I had been accepted!

"I'm in, Mama, I'm in!" I cried, jumping up and down in her place like a deranged person. "Let's get on our knees!"

We knelt in the middle of the living room floor and bowed our heads, giving thanks to God. Mama kept smiling and shaking her head, as if in a state of disbelief. Then the tears started flowing down her cheeks.

"Lord have mercy, Lord have mercy. I don't believe it, I just don't believe it. Thank you, Jesus, thank you, Jesus."

Thank you, Jesus, indeed. Because there was no other explanation for why I was now college-bound, after having spent most of my life speeding toward self-destruction.

As Mama continued to cry, I thought to myself, See, Mama, I'm on my road to redemption. I've saved your life.

To my way of thinking, she was still alive because I was keeping the pact I had made with God. Her hair was thinning slightly and she had lost about thirty pounds. But the important thing was that she was still alive. I was propelling her forward, willing her to live through undertaking a fundamental change in my behavior. I was holding up my end of the bargain and God was holding up His.

The icing on the cake came that Saturday in Mama's Seventh-Day Adventist Church. The preacher asked everybody who was headed to college in the fall to please stand up and state what school they were attending. There was a distinct murmur in the church when I proudly rose from my pew, not to mention more than a few looks of astonishment.

As if that wasn't enough, I was going to the most prestigious school of all the young people who stood up!

When the time came to register for classes, my oldest brother, Ron, rode out to Eastern Michigan with me. Whereas Addison had been upbeat, Ron took on his trademark, mildly pessimistic approach.

"You gotta leave behind that life you used to live," he said quietly as soon as we got into his car. "If you had really applied yourself, you could have gone to a better school." Ron is the kind of guy that if you told him you had just won ten million dollars in the lotto, he'd tick off the potential downsides.

I used to resent the hell out of his sobering take on the world, but in time I came to appreciate where he was coming from.

Eastern Michigan gave me some financial aid but not enough to cover all my expenses. As Addison had suggested, I would have to work my way through college. When I told this to Dale, my manager at McDonald's, he allowed me to start working a six P.M. to one A.M. shift. I would still be working five days a week, but only three week-days now.

From the time I was accepted at Eastern Michigan until the first day of classes, I walked around feeling ecstatic. But from time to time, self-doubt crept into the picture, too. I had proven that I could survive in a world where you needed mother wit, guile, and ruthlessness to survive. Did I have what it took to prosper at Eastern Michigan?

Full of swagger and bravado on the outside, inwardly I really didn't know if I could cut it. I mean, let's get real—I had a friggin' GED, while many of Eastern Michigan's students had attended elite prep schools. I wasn't sure how I would fare against them, but the important thing was that I was eager to find out.

The day before I started college, I made sure that I would remain grounded while at Eastern Michigan, if nothing else. I accomplished that by hooking up with my boys back at Herman Gardens.

"Ain't this a bitch!" they shouted, aware that I was headed off to college and surprised I would still seek out my homies. "What's up, Joe College? You slummin'?"

If they had any doubts as to whether I was still down, those disappeared the moment I pulled a fat joint from my pocket and fired that sucker up. That's how I spent the Sunday before my first day of college—smoking weed and drinking wine with people I believed would always have my back whether I was in an ivory tower or on death row.

I was well anesthetized after hanging out with the fellas, so I had no trouble drifting off to sleep that night. When my alarm clock jarred me awake at six A.M., I hopped out of bed immediately, eager to begin the day.

What do you wear on your first day of college? This was something I had never discussed with Addison or Ronald. So I put on my sharpest suit and drove to Eastern Michigan toting an expensive briefcase I had purchased for the occasion.

I thought about Eastern Michigan's coeds the entire time I was driving there. Would they be standoffish after finding out about my background?

The other thing on my mind as I drove west on I-94 was my mother. It made me feel damn good to know that for once she was bursting with pride because of me, instead of cringing with shame. For once I was bringing her happiness, instead of pain and frustration and embarrassment.

When I reached campus, cars were lined up bumper to bumper and creeping along at about 2 mph. I was shocked to see that virtually no one, except for me, was dressed up for the first day of school. In fact, it seemed that everyone had on bummy-looking jeans and T-shirts, while I looked like a stylish corporate lawyer. I immediately felt totally out of place.

After I got out of my car, I noticed that the student body appeared to be 90 percent white and that most of the white kids looked through me instead of at me. The black students, on the other hand, appeared to see me but were hard-pressed to utter a word of greeting. I may have thought the suit I was wearing was sharp, but they immediately took in how cheaply made it was and also noticed the street mannerisms that were part of my package.

They wanted no part of a brother from the streets and wasted no time communicating that.

I was tremendously disappointed to learn that a bunch of fake-ass, self-important Negroes were attending Eastern Michigan!

What kind of weird *Alice in Wonderland* shit is this, and where do I fit in here? Do I even *want* to fit in?

If push came to shove, I knew I could always hang out at nearby Washtenaw Community College. My friend from Peterson Academy, Andre, was going to school there, along with some other brothers we knew from Peterson and the Seventh-Day Adventist Church. At least we could band together and keep it real, instead of running around acting all cold and plastic.

As for dealing with Eastern Michigan's students, I started doing something I do whenever I feel rejected—I confronted their rejection with arrogance. "You people think you're too good for me? Okay, here's an invitation to kiss my ass, then!"

As I looked for the building where my first class was to convene, I continued to swagger about Eastern Michigan's campus and began mirroring the indifference I felt from the students there. "Fuck all y'all!"

When I made it to my classroom, frankly I was shocked. It was held in one of those cavernous auditorium classrooms that held endless rows of seats. There had to be two hundred students crammed in there!

The professor gave each of us a syllabus and began lecturing about his expectations, the assignments we had to complete, and the dates when tests would be administered. I was like, "Wow, this is cool!" I liked being told right up front what was expected of me. I immediately began formulating a plan to jump ahead of the other students in the class by completing all the assignments before they were due. I badly wanted to show my standoffish counterparts that I was smarter than all of them.

Before the first week of school was over, my crew from Washtenaw Community College began making their presence felt on Eastern Michigan's campus. Naturally, I fell right in with them. We'd usually gather at the student union building to ogle co-eds.

Showing that it's really hard for a leopard to change its spots, we'd occasionally steal steaks from grocery stores surrounding Eastern Michigan, or walk out of nearby restaurants without paying. Don't ask me why, because I had everything to lose and nothing to gain from doing dumb shit like that. All I can say is, peer pressure can sometimes be a bitch.

Despite those lapses, I was a serious student and attacked my schoolwork with vigor. I had four courses: political science, history, English, and remedial algebra.

I was in college! I chuckled to myself every time I entered Eastern Michigan's beautiful campus.

"I fooled y'all. I ain't supposed to be here, but here I am, world!"

I was commuting between Eastern Michigan and Wayne every morning Monday through Thursday and was working full time. It didn't take long to see that juggling those activities and dealing with my commute called for a level of commitment and focus I had never summoned before in my life.

Back home, worrisome developments were starting to materialize. Mama had lost a lot more weight and had begun to wear a wig because her hair was coming out in clumps due to her chemotherapy treatments. She was nauseated most of the time, hadn't worked in months, and was spending most of her day at home watching soap operas.

In fact, her health had deteriorated to the point where Addison's mother, Aunt Ethel, had begun taking care of Mama in the afternoons. My mother was becoming less and less mobile and spending more and more time in bed.

Even though I had to take her to the hospital in a wheelchair a couple of times, I still convinced myself that her problems stemmed from her medical treatments and that as soon as they were completed, she would be back to her old self.

Toward the beginning of October, I was delighted to realize a professional goal I had been working hard for: I was promoted to full assistant manager at the McDonald's where I was employed.

I wasted little time sharing this with Mama. She was lying in her bed and was so ill by that time that she only gave my news a lukewarm response, instead of the hearty congratulations I had been anticipating.

"That's good, baby, that's good," she said, giving a smile that was more of a grimace due to her pain. "Keep on going."

Remembering how robust and lively she had been most of my life, it was now somewhat disheartening to see and speak with my mother. Every time I saw evidence of her decline, it loosened the wall of denial I had painstakingly constructed.

"It's just her treatments," I kept telling myself. "Once they're finished, she'll be fine."

Then I would eagerly dive back into my responsibilities at Eastern Michigan and at McDonald's, glad those demanding endeavors kept me from focusing on much else.

This probably won't come as much of a surprise, but after a while the demands of working full-time and attending college full-time began to kick my ass. I had to prioritize, something new for me. The first activity I dropped from my schedule was the dope smoking and partying I occasionally did with my boys after getting off from McDonald's at night.

That decision may sound quite adult and responsible, but it really had more to do with self-preservation than anything else. A terrifying ordeal I experienced one day after class played a major role in my decision.

I had driven from Eastern Michigan to Romulus to work at McDonald's, then driven several miles west of the city, to Ypsilanti, for a little partying with my Washtenaw Community College posse.

I left my boys around three o'clock in the morning, headed back home, to Wayne. I must have dozed off, because I was suddenly aware that my car was in the middle of a curve, going about 40 mph, and headed directly toward a huge wooden utility pole.

I had about half a second to brace myself before the car smashed into that monstrous obstacle with an obscenely hard impact. One minute I was driving along; the next I was seeing stars, sitting in a car that had steam billowing from beneath its badly mangled front end. Although I was disoriented, I still had enough presence of mind to hop out of my car, fearing that it might burst into flames.

I started to shake a few minutes later, realizing that I could easily have been killed in that accident, which totaled my car.

Mama started letting me use her white Oldsmobile Cutlass, because she wasn't driving much at that point. Not too long after my run-in with the utility pole, Mama began to complain of stomach pains and was moaning in a way that scared me to death, so I took her to Henry Ford Hospital, where she was admitted.

A stout woman when her health was good, Mama had dropped to 130 pounds. Her head was usually drooped to one side when I visited her and she was practically always sedated. When I told her that I had qualified for a grant at Eastern Michigan based on my lack of income, she just stared at me with dull eyes that contained no spark of recognition.

The handwriting was on the wall. I refused to see it. I attributed her dramatic setback to the medicine they were giving her, in an award-winning example of the human mind's refusal to acknowledge something readily apparent, but painful.

However, whenever my brothers and I looked at each other inside Henry Ford Hospital, you could see from our eyes and our expressions that we all knew Mama's time had come. Nobody was willing to admit that, though.

Ultimately, she began to ease in and out of a coma. That went on for a couple of days, until I got a call one night when I was working the late shift at McDonald's. The somber voice on the line belonged to Addison.

"I think you may need to get down here to the hospital, man," he said without mincing any words. "It doesn't look good."

My three brothers and I dutifully assembled at my mother's

bedside inside Henry Ford Hospital. All four of us were scared to death, even Ron.

Mama had moved out of her coma and into some kind of weird state where she was experiencing hallucinations.

"Look at that mouse!" she cried out in an agitated voice. "Somebody get that mouse! Now!"

Stunned, my brothers and I awkwardly tried to reassure our mother.

"You're going to be all right, Mama, you're going to be all right."

Just like that, a moment of lucidity came over our mom. "You boys keep going to church, okay?" she croaked in a barely audible voice. "And stay together and look out for each other."

I don't think anyone said a word because we would have collapsed in sobs. My mother had been my entire world, and I was spiraling down into an emotional whirlpool that words really can't do justice to. Anyone who's ever lost their mom knows what I'm talking about.

When the end finally came on October 21, 1978, I was in a Henry Ford Hospital waiting room. One of the medical workers came out and said, "Your mother passed. She's no longer suffering."

My temper detonated at that instant and I felt an overwhelming urge to take my foot and ram it in the middle of God's two-timing ass.

The Creator and I had entered into an explicit contract: I would stop acting like a hooligan and clean up my act in return for my mother's continued existence. I had held up my end of the bargain in exemplary fashion and God had responded by taking Mama!

I was mad as hell and doubted whether there really was a God. That's what raged through my brain as the quiet sound of Steve's crying reverberated inside the waiting room.

Somebody asked if I was okay, and I took that as my cue to hurriedly depart the hospital. I wanted everyone to leave me the fuck alone.

I didn't get involved at all in planning Mama's funeral. That task was primarily handled by Ron and my aunt Ethel, my mother's sister. The funeral was held at the Detroit Seventh-Day Adventist church I had grown up in, and the ceremony was humble and quiet, as my mother would have wished.

To be honest, I don't remember an awful lot of it with the exception of walking down the aisle when I entered the church. Everyone who gazed at me looked so pitiful and sorrowful that I could almost feel my energy and spirit being drawn from my body.

During the funeral service, my emotions careened wildly between anger and sorrow.

When my mother was driven to her final resting place at Gethsemane Cemetery in Detroit, I refused to watch as her casket was lowered into the ground. Nor did I speak to anyone as the black funeral limo drove us back to Mama's place.

At that point in time, Addison was going through a divorce, so he was staying at Mama's town home, as was Steve. In retrospect, I'm glad they were there. I don't think I could have handled being alone.

Her death didn't seem real to me, but for a full year after she died I dreamed about her every single night. I talked to her about things that were happening in my life and was still able to get her counsel.

Addison couldn't help but notice my foul mood in the weeks that followed Mama's passing. I was sullen, only spoke when spoken to, and went out of my way to avoid contact with people. One day Addison pulled my coattail on it.

"Just pray, man, just pray," he counseled me.

"Pray for what?" I shot back heatedly. "That's what I had been doing, but doesn't seem like that's doing much, does it? I prayed to God to change my life and save my mother's life—I turned my life around, but he didn't save her life."

Addison looked back at me with a blank expression. I rose to leave, because I didn't feel like listening to whatever else he had to say.

"Hold on one second, Greg," he said mildly. "God doesn't make deals, okay? That isn't how God operates."

I walked out of the room, thinking, Yeah, yeah, man. I ain't trying to hear you Holy Rollers these days. I've been double-crossed, so just shut up.

Our conversation didn't help me much at that particular moment, but as time went on it began to make a lot of sense. And as I continued to dream about my mother, eventually I became convinced that God was putting those visions there to comfort me.

My sixth-grade class picture at
Peterson Academy

Brothers Ron and Kenneth in the
Herman Gardens housing project,
Christmas 1973

Brother Steve in his first bachelor
pad, the following year

With Linda in our
early days

Walking up the aisle
on our wedding day,
June 1, 1985

Speaking at
Operation PUSH in
Detroit about our
1986 Revlon boycott

Presenting former
congressman Bill
Gray with the
Detroit city council
resolution regarding
his congressional
achievements

On the campaign
trail with Jesse
Jackson during his
1988 presidential
run. I managed his
Detroit operation.

One of the proudest days of my life: graduating from law school in 1987

With boss and mentor Councilman Clyde Cleveland at a dinner celebrating my graduation

Working with Free South Africa leader Randall Robinson in Washington, DC, in 1989

At a 1989 fundraiser with Detroit mayor Coleman Young.

Celebrating my election victory with lifelong friends Sanford Kelly, Craig Lewis, and Rick Jones

Being sworn in as judge for the 36th district of Michigan

Linda and the kids join me on my first day on the bench

With my cousin and mentor Addison Hines and Reverend Greer

With the staff and members of Young Adults Asserting Themselves, the youth agency I founded, in 1986

With mentor Annette Rainwater and Jesse Jackson, Jr.

Being honored by the Southern Christian Leadership Conference with national chairman Dr. Claud Young and event chair Robin Barclay

Visiting the old neighbor-hood: on Prairie Street with Mattie Fears and Anthony Fears

With my brother Kenneth, our kids, nieces, and nephews on vacation in 2000

Hanging out at home with Linda and from left, daughter Jade, son Greg Jr., daughter Camara, son Amir, and dog Tuffy

My mother, the incredible Alice Mathis

VIII

PICK A CARD, ANY CARD!

During the 1979 spring semester at Eastern Michigan, I quit my job at McDonald's. Juggling a full-time work load and full-time academic load was just too much to handle. Plus I had a C-minus average, meaning that I was on academic probation. I could always go back to McDonald's, but my first priority was to get my average up.

Thanks to an insurance policy of Mama's I had a couple thousand dollars to work with. Still, you can never have enough money, it seems. To make a little extra, I started working as a deejay at campus parties. Not only did that put a little extra scratch in my pocket, it allowed me to become quite popular with the black students on campus.

Along with one of my buddies from Washtenaw Community College, Lamont, I introduced disco to Eastern Michigan's student body, leading my boys to nickname me "Scoey," a derivation of disco.

Lamont and I used to promote parties and charge students five bucks to get in. Remaining true to my Detroit roots, I could be found around campus decked out in a gold chain, big glasses, a shirt open to my navel, bell bottoms, and high, high platform-heel shoes.

I was delighted to have finally found a niche.

However, when the summer rolled around and Eastern Michigan's students went home on break, my disco business dried up. That put me back in familiar territory, namely hard economic times.

Once again, my Washtenaw Community College buddies rode to the rescue. They may have been in Ypsilanti instead of Detroit, but Andre and the boys were finding that being involved in petty theft and selling light drugs were still effective ways to make money.

I was still trying to battle the lure of the streets, but a growling, empty stomach has a way of pushing aside honorable intentions. So the next time I received one of the Social Security checks I was getting because of my father, me and the Washtenaw crew used it to buy some reefer.

We rolled the reefer into joints that we sold for a dollar apiece. I did this in the vicinity of Eastern Michigan but never on campus, because I didn't want to damage my image.

We also did little credit card scams; we would order things illegally through the mail, then sell them. Friends who worked in retail outlets and restaurants scribbled down credit card numbers and expiration dates, and gave them to us. Andre and I rented a vacant off-campus apartment and we had the merchandise sent to it.

I think one of the things that drew me to Andre and him to me was that we both had towering ambition. But while I still had aspirations of going legit and staying that way, Andre wanted no part of the straight life. Not satisfied with the money we were making from our nickel-and-dime operations, he hooked up a connection with one of the drug-dealing gangs in Detroit to sell heroin.

It was an extremely profitable thing to get into back then. Mere kids were making a thousand dollars a week, and the gang leaders were gladly supplying them with 9-mm guns. Around 1979, it was as if an evil sorcerer magically flooded Detroit's black neighborhoods with an avalanche of guns and drugs.

Andre approached me and asked if I had any interest in selling heroin with him. Satan has an uncanny way of testing your strongest convictions. I still wasn't quite sure where I stood with God at that phase in my life, and I was impressed by the money that was being generated by the heroin gangs.

How sincere was I about trying to go legit?

Rather than make a snap decision about something that could easily determine what happened with the rest of my life, I put Andre off. I told him I would mull it over and get back to him.

I sought the advice of an old friend from my Herman Gardens days, Rick, who had been to jail for selling heroin a few years earlier and had just been released from prison. When I told him about Andre's proposal, Rick emphatically warned me to stay out of the heroin game. He also reminded me how far I had come and what I had promised my mother.

We were sitting inside his car with the windows down and the air conditioner off, laughing at little black kids playing in a fire hydrant not far from where I used to live at Herman Gardens. Although we were making light chitchat, Rick could sense something was gnawing at me.

"What the fuck's up, boy?" he said, gesturing for me to hand him a cigarette. Rolling my eyes, I shook one out of the pack as the kids squealed with delight. I kind of envied their ability to just enjoy life without a care in the world. After years of dying to be old, here I was wishing to be young.

"Brotherman, I am struggling my ass off financially," I replied to Rick with a laugh. "Times are tight, man."

"Yeah, that's what college students do," Rick shot back without a trace of a smile. "They struggle, man. That's the name of the game."

After that conversation, I told Andre that I would continue to sell reefer and do credit card stuff, but I wasn't entering the heroin game. Not only did that decision create a rift in our relationship, it led to an uncomfortable rivalry.

"Oh, you gonna punk out, huh?" Andre asked, sneering. "You probably ain't got the heart for it. This is a whole new level of game, so you go on and stick with that college thing. I'm gonna go make me some money."

I didn't feel I had a damn thing to prove to Andre or anybody else, so his goading had no affect on me. Except to piss me off. We had been through so much, going back to our days in church school, that he knew what I was capable of.

A couple members of the Washtenaw Community College crew decided to make the quantum leap with Andre. So did a brother named Vincent, who had attended the Peterson Academy with Andre and me. That move would later prove to be Vincent's undoing.

After I told Andre that I had no desire to clock heroin with him, he treated me like I was less than an equal—a hanger-on, a lame. That hurt me, because Andre was my boy from way back. We were so close that I had slept at his place in Detroit several nights that summer.

But most of my nights were spent in the home of my oldest brother, Ron, who was living in a comfortable neighborhood on Detroit's East Side by that time. Seeing that I was sincere about trying to turn my life around, he had allowed me to move in with him and his wife. They kindly set aside their guestroom, which was the spot where I laid my head.

When the fall semester of my sophomore year got under way, I was able to give academics my undivided attention for the second semester in a row, because I was no longer working full time. Even so, I was still earning Cs in the math and business classes.

That served as a reality check for me, because there was no way I could continue to do that and get out of Eastern Michigan with a degree in business administration. After a good deal of thought I just concluded that, hey, I'm not the best at everything.

So I went to Eastern Michigan's library and got a book listing different career options. The book strongly recommended that students pick careers in areas in which they excelled and in which there would be employment opportunities.

One section of the book had a little aptitude test to determine what fields you might do well in. Based on my scores, it looked as though I might have a future as a lawyer, schoolteacher, or social worker, all areas that dealt with the social sciences. Naturally, my ambition led me to want to shoot for attorney. Malcolm X had wanted to be a lawyer, so that further intensified my desire.

With this goal in mind, I switched my major to public administration, which has to do with running public businesses, whether a nonprofit or government agency. I made that switch with an eye toward applying to law school after earning my four-year degree.

The decision paid immediate dividends in terms of my grades, which shot up to As and Bs, to my delight. I still wasn't crazy about classes that had anything to do with math, but got a kick out of world history, political science, psychology, and sociology. I liked these classes because they helped me develop a worldview and also helped explain the dichotomy between rich people and poor people.

In addition to myself, there were four other college hustlers who decided it would be best not to follow Andre into the heroin trade. One of them, who went by the name of Stone, devised a three-card monte scam that he and I began to run on Eastern Michigan's campus during my second year.

I was the barker who attracted suckers to our site, while Stone was the straight man who appeared to step from the audience and immediately start to win money. We began running this ancient scam in the student union, atop one of the pool tables.

In no time ten or twelve students would gather around as I vigorously shuffled three cards that were turned facedown—two of them clubs, one a heart—and challenge Stone to flip over the red card.

To the uninitiated, it sure seemed that Stone was winning anywhere from ten to twenty dollars per hand, while I was growing increasingly annoyed with his uncanny ability to flip over the red card.

"Pick the red card," I cried, sweating slightly from the exertion of zipping three cards back and forth across the playing surface of a pool table. "I've got two black kings and one red king here, folks. Step on up and pick the red card and win your lunch money. Keep your eye on the cards, though. Because if you don't, I get paid."

At that point, Stone eagerly reached for what he knew damn well was a black card and flipped it over.

"Ooooh, black king," I said, feigning disappointment. "Money gone. Next. Who's gonna be next. How about you—you look kinda slick. Where you from, the city?"

That comment was directed toward a naïve-looking brother who stepped up to the pool table and slapped a five-dollar bill on it. I was chuckling inside, because that boy had "easy money" written all over him. The five-spot he laid on the pool table was as good as mine.

"I knew you were a city slicker," I yelled, swirling the three cards twice as fast as when Stone had been playing. I slid the cards around the pool table surface for a good minute, then stopped so the sucker could pick a black one and I could pocket his five dollars.

He was about to make his decision when some wide-eyed, middle-class black co-ed, who didn't have a dime in the game, walked up to the pool table bold as could be and coolly flipped over the red card!

I began cursing her out from A to Z, calling that meddling hussy everything but a child of God. "Bitch, what the fuck is wrong with you? You ain't got no goddamned money down here! Is you crazy?"

"Yeah, but I see what you're doing," she replied hotly, "and your boy over there who keeps winning the money is working *with you*!"

The crowd let out a collective, "Ohhhhh!"

Thinking fast and seeking to deflect attention away from myself, I begin to cuss out the innocent-looking young thing whose big-ass mouth had ruined the nice thing Stone and I had going.

Another black co-ed who was with Miss Meddlesome vigorously leaped to her defense. "Man, leave her alone," she screamed. "Come on, Linda!"

With that, Stone and I quickly packed up our tent and left the student union before somebody called the campus police.

"Damn, man, how did she figure that shit out?" Stone asked, glaring in the girl's general direction as we walked out the door. "That square broad."

"Oh well, fuck it," I said, mentally calculating how much money I would need to make it through the week. "That's the end of that. Maybe we'll see that simple ho again."

I did see her again a couple of days later, and I felt bad for publicly showering the sister with profanity. That was a foul thing to do, despite her stupid move. I felt doubly bad once I noticed how fine she was.

Girlfriend had it going on, with hazel eyes, brown skin, long hair, and a slammin' body. I was with Stone once again, and when she saw the two of us, she immediately turned toward one of her friends and began whispering animatedly. Suddenly she turned toward me.

"What are y'all doing up here, anyway?" she asked sharply, glowering. "This is a college!"

Now I was offended.

"What do you mean, what am I doing here?" I said with a curtness that equaled hers. "I go to school here. I'm a junior and I'm doing good."

"Yeah, right!"

Since I was the one who'd displayed the nasty, ignorant mouth and not Stone, he started rapping to our inquisitor's friend. Meanwhile, I sort of hung back, because the little card shark looked like she wanted to kill me.

Stone and the co-ed he had been talking to really hit it off and he arranged to have a rendezvous at her dormitory the next day, so I tagged along. The young lady who'd interrupted my three-card monte was also there, sitting at a desk and diligently attacking her homework. When she saw me, she scowled and said, "I'll be back."

Then she gathered up her books and stomped off. I followed her to the lounge area, intrigued by this feisty young woman.

"So, what's your name, baby?"

"It's not bitch!" she snapped.

"Baby, why don't you let me take you shopping to make up for all that nasty stuff I said to you?" I made a point of taking out my bankroll, which may have been a few hundred dollars, and counting off some bills.

"What are you—some kind of thug or something? Is that money you took from people with your crooked game? I still don't know what you're doing up here!"

"Hey, look, I said I was sorry. A brother's got to make a living, baby. What's your name, girl?"

"Linda Reese."

Linda Reese didn't have much conversation for me that day, which I understood. The next time I saw her, I was delighted that I had some of my textbooks with me.

"See, I got my books with me. I'm a student here. In fact, I'm getting As and Bs."

"Whatever," Linda said, steadily walking in the opposite direction and looking appalled to have run into me. It was time to go for the sympathy move.

"Look, the only reason I'm trying to hustle is because I don't have a mother and father. My mother and father didn't buy me a new car, and I ain't from the suburbs." The words were flowing now. "So you gonna let me take you shopping? Come on, let me take you to dinner and then shopping."

Linda thought about this for a moment before uttering a reluctant yes. That was all I needed to hear.

I drove her to a mall in Ann Arbor, Michigan, that had a movie theater, but I was smart enough not to bring up that shopping nonsense again. We watched a flick together and I spent a lot of time sneaking glances at Linda. I really wanted to lean over and kiss her, with her soft-looking skin and sexy perfume, but I knew that wouldn't go over too well after the way that we'd met.

So I kept my hands to myself and was able to score some points by making little quiet comments about the movie that made Linda laugh. To be honest, I didn't want the movie to end, because I knew she would want to immediately return to her dormitory and do something boring like homework. I, on the other hand, had different ideas about how we might spend the rest of the evening.

When the movie ended and the final credits began to roll, I very reluctantly rose from my seat and escorted Linda from the darkened movie theater. After I drove her back to campus she wouldn't let me enter her dorm, which I expected. However, she did give me a little peck on the cheek, which I found encouraging, and we exchanged phone numbers.

I called her about an hour later.

"Hey. How you doin'?" I said in my best mack-daddy voice. "I made it home safely, so I just called so you wouldn't worry about me."

"Oh Greg," Linda said, laughing. I silently pumped my fist. If you can make a woman swoon or laugh, you've got a leg up on the competition.

In the days after our little movie date, I found myself becoming more and more attracted to Linda. For one thing, I admired the way she stood up to me and exposed my scam when I was running my three-card monte. I can intimidate most people, but Linda didn't seem fazed by me in the least.

She was also very independent and had a pretty fair degree of black consciousness, unlike the vast majority of black students at Eastern Michigan. We continued to go out on little dates and after about a month or so officially became boyfriend and girlfriend.

Linda took me to meet her parents, who lived in Oak Park, a sub-urb of Detroit that was predominantly Jewish at the time.

I gulped when I saw the house Linda grew up in—it was fancier than any house I had ever set foot in. Just like the first time I came on to Eastern Michigan's campus, I was hit with an urge to turn around and call the whole thing off.

My palms were moist and my stomach was tight over the prospect of meeting Linda's father, an engineer with the phone company, and her mother, an administrator, because I expected them to be snooty and to make me feel ill at ease.

But they were very down-to-earth and I had a wonderful, relaxed time. Linda's two older sisters weren't there when I met her parents, but I eventually got to meet them, too.

Like me, Linda was serious about her schoolwork, so that made it a lot easier to park my buns in the boring library hour after boring hour. That was something I needed to do.

As I began my junior year, I was feeling pressure to get my grade point average up if I was to have any chance of getting into law school.

But college is about more than books, and my junior year was when I began to delve into extracurricular activities at Eastern Michigan. I didn't join any of the fraternities, because they seemed to be more into screwing girls and throwing parties than anything else. Instead, I joined the College Democrats and became something of a campus activist. The Free South Africa movement was in high gear and it came to my attention that South African golfer Gary Player was to play golf with Eastern Michigan's alumni association.

To protest this, I arranged a campus demonstration in front of the student administration building that about one hundred students showed up for, an unusually high number. I followed that up with three more protest demonstrations, but the university's administration still would not relent.

So I put together a massive protest march attended by roughly one thousand students, some from the University of Michigan. Seeing that many students passionately address a social inequity, and knowing that it was because of me, gave me a huge charge. I felt that I had done something worthy of Jesse Jackson or Malcolm X.

That demonstration got plenty of media coverage, too. I certainly got the administration's attention, but they held their Gary Player outing anyway.

In the spring semester of my junior year, I decided to run for president of the campus NAACP chapter. The street guys I used to run with on campus were having less and less to do with me by this point, because they'd come to see me as a campus square.

It's funny how your self-perception and the way others see you can be light years apart. I would learn that lesson in a very painful way one day, after leaving Eastern Michigan's campus for Detroit so I could check in on the homeboys at the Herman Gardens housing project.

As soon as I got there, I immediately ran into four former gang members I used to beg, borrow, and steal with back in the day. They either reeked of alcohol or had the listless appearance of someone strung out on heroin.

An odd thought ran through my mind as I hugged my former crew and exchanged elaborate handshakes that only we knew—I used to think that being a junkie was cool! But at the moment, it struck me as a senseless waste of human potential.

Believe it or not, the portico I used to hang out on was still there, only now its wooden structure was unpainted and broken down, and the odor of urine had it stinking to high heaven. Shards of broken glass glittered everywhere, something I never saw when I first moved to Herman Gardens.

Despite the forced joviality of my longtime hanging partners, they seemed to lack the energy and the life force I recalled from our younger days. They seemed broken in spirit and cynical about life and everything it had to offer. They had resigned themselves to being at the bottom of the socioeconomic ladder forever, living for that next high and resorting to odd jobs and petty crime to tide themselves over.

Still, I didn't feel out of place, nor did I look down on my boys. Because there but for the grace of almighty God—and Mama's guidance—went I.

So we sat on the portico kicking it, talking about old times and running down the list of our boys who were incarcerated, crippled, or dead. Thinking that maybe my Herman Gardens friends needed a little spark, I started trying to sell them on college life. I related that getting a college degree could open a lot of doors and that if I could get my bad ass into college, anybody could.

My efforts to motivate and inspire did not go over well. Maybe I came off as preachy, although I don't think I did. In any event, my boys began to testily contradict and ridicule practically everything I had to say about college and the opportunities it opened up.

After being beat down by life at every turn, they didn't want to entertain any fairy tales about beautiful college campuses filled with foxy co-eds, carefree student life, or good-paying gigs that magically materialized after graduation.

"We ain't trying to hear that shit, man," one of my boys said so sarcastically and meanly that I turned to him in surprise. "How we gonna get into some goddamned college when we ain't even graduated from high school? What kinda fantasy shit is that?"

I held up my hand, signaling for him to back off. "Yo, man, this shit is on the real. This ya boy Scoey you talkin' to. I ain't here to bullshit you."

"Man, fuck all dat shit and fuck dem whities, too, because we don't want to be a part of it," someone else chimed up. "Matter of fact . . . give up some of that shit you got on."

With that, two members of my crew slid pistols out of their pants and pointed them at me! I could tell from the sullen, hard expressions of my boys that they were not playing.

"Whassup?" I said, forcing a laugh. "Y'all—why you frontin' on me and shit?"

A guy named Fernando helped break it down for me by busting me upside my head with his piece. I still have the scar on my head to this day. Then three of the guys started pistol-whipping me on the portico, in full view of everyone who happened to be in Herman Gardens. Everybody knew that if the police questioned a potential witness, he or she would turn out to be blind—and deaf, too.

Those fools jacked me for my wallet, a nice two-piece sweatsuit I had on, the jacket I was wearing, and my watch and jewelry. Adding insult to injury, those muthafuckas even snatched my new Adidas tennis shoes, leaving me in my stocking feet. For some reason, though, they stopped short of taking my car keys.

"You best stay yo' ass up there with them little college honkies," they warned as they walked away laughing, leisurely counting my bankroll.

After years of operating as a ruthless hunter, showing neither remorse nor pity for my victims, now I was the prey. And it was my own wolf pack that had turned on me.

I remained perched on a broken-down wooden bench on the portico, dressed in my underwear and gym socks and not even bothering to dab at the blood flowing from my head. A couple of people came running up to console me, furious about what they had seen.

"Hey, that's some fucked-up shit—you want us to get 'em for you, man?"

I shook my head no and finally got up to leave the portico. Pride and respect had been the main motivating factors in my life and now here I was walking around Herman Gardens half-naked and bleeding after having been rolled. I went to the housing unit of a family I knew, called my friend Rick on the telephone, and indignantly related what had just gone down.

"My boys can be there in half an hour," Rick said belligerently. "Just say the word and this shit is ON."

All I had to do was say yes and at least one of my attackers would be lying in a pool of his own blood by nightfall. Detroit was at a point in its history where it was being called the nation's Murder Capital, and there was no shortage of brothers who would eagerly waste my antagonists in return for a pinch of heroin or coke.

A few years earlier, I might have tracked down all four of them myself and capped them. But I had had enough of African American males disrespecting and destroying each other.

"Rick, man, just let it go."

I was inside the home of a lady named B. J. Knight, who said the guys who'd rolled me were suspected of a couple of neighborhood murders and had been barging into the housing units of elderly women and raping them.

"See, that's why folks don't come back once they make it out of here," Mrs. Knight said, pressing a wet washcloth against my temple. "Don't do anything that will make you go to jail now, baby."

After pretending for a week or two that I intended to get retribution, I allowed my experience at Herman Gardens to fade into the background and stopped talking about it. Pure and simple, I wasn't a gangster anymore. I finally had to accept that.

In retrospect, my boys did me a favor by showing me that I had to choose between being a gangster or a college professional.

Still, a lot of my manhood was tied up in street culture. I felt down and depressed because I sensed that I was losing a part of myself.

However, all my life I've had a way of converting negative feelings and situations into positive motivation. In time, getting robbed at Herman Gardens became an I'm-gonna-show-them event for me.

With that in mind, I focused all my energy and determination toward Eastern Michigan's campus, where it belonged.

Over the next year and a half, my whole life was wrapped up in campus politics and in getting decent grades. So it was gratifying to keep getting As and Bs, not to mention being elected president of the College Democrats and president of the Public Administration Society.

I tried to get President Jimmy Carter to speak at a campus event, but failed in that effort. However, I did manage to snag Carter's chief of staff, Hamilton Jordon.

When an election cycle came around for state legislators and judges, I persuaded them to hold campus rallies to articulate their views on various issues. Politics is basically the art of accumulating power and wielding it effectively, and I found myself fascinated by the process.

On a sunny day in May 1982, I graduated with the rest of my class, even though I was a few credits short of my degree and needed to attend one final class in the fall.

My brothers Ron and Steve were there for my graduation, along with Mama's sister, Aunt Ethel, and Linda and her parents. My cousin Addison was there, too, with tears in his eyes.

"Your mother would be so proud of you!" he kept repeating over and over in the campus fieldhouse where the graduation ceremony was held. "You did it."

Grinning, I thanked Addison, then quickly changed the subject because if he mentioned Mama one more time, I would lose it, too. I felt my mother's joyous presence as I walked across the stage in my graduation robe, the proud recipient of a B.S. degree in public administration. Whenever I do something noteworthy, I feel a strong connection to Mama that makes me feel as though she and I have achieved my victory as one.

When all the pomp and circumstance and backslapping were over, I peered through the packed, steamy fieldhouse, desperately searching for Addison's face. Aside from Mama, more than anyone he appreciated the incredible transformation I had undergone.

Clutching my diploma, I finally spotted Addison in the huge, festive crowd and raced toward him, beaming like a madman. I gave my dear cousin, who had presented me with encouragement and love as long as I could remember, a hard bear hug. We were both crying as we embraced, appreciating that my presence at Eastern Michigan University that day was nothing short of an inner city miracle.

It marked the first time I had wept since Mama's death four years earlier.

IX

LOVE CHILD

I was so in love with politics by the summer of 1982 that I figured it made sense to see if I could get plugged into Detroit's political scene.

So I donned a suit and tie and traveled down to the city council, intent on bopping into the place and meeting the council president, just like that. Walking in off the street with no appointment isn't the best way to get face time with powerful urban politicians. But I was able to meet with Art Bowman, one of the council president's aides.

When I told Bowman I was available to work a paid or an unpaid internship, he appeared to be impressed. Most college students don't have the foresight to recognize that the knowledge gained and contacts made while working for nothing may soon prove worth their weight in gold.

All the while, though, I was secretly praying that a paid internship was available. Lord knows I needed the scratch, because I was living with Ron and working at a McDonald's as an assistant manager until my single fall class started.

"Unfortunately there are no positions available–paid or unpaid," Bowman said.

My shoulders drooped visibly on hearing that news.

Bowman noticed the look of disappointment that swept over my face. "Okay," he said. "If you don't mind coming here to work for free, I'll show you the ropes around this place."

True to his word, Bowman allowed me to come into Detroit's city council twice a week and take a seat behind him in council chambers. By the time our arrangement got under way, Eastern Michigan's fall semester had begun and I was taking the class I needed for my diploma, as well as two master's level courses.

Mama's white Oldsmobile Cutlass had given up the ghost long ago, so I was without transportation. To make my deal with Bowman work, I had to take a bus from Ypsilanti, Michigan, where Eastern Michigan was located, to Detroit twice a week. It was an hour and a half Greyhound bus ride to cover the 120-mile round trip. But the inconvenience seemed like a small price to pay in light of what I was getting in return.

Bowman started me out slowly, giving me gofer-level responsibilities to take care of. When he saw that I was eager and dependable, then heavier responsibilities began to come. He began to allow me to research ordinances that concerned issues coming before the council. I began to spend a lot of time in the law library on the tenth floor of the City Hall office building.

In a word, I found Detroit politics and the interaction between city politicians fascinating. I felt I was a part of something that was really relevant, especially given the fact that Detroit has a mostly black population.

I was happily flying around the City Hall complex twice a week, decked out in granny glasses and a cheap navy blue blazer with sleeves that were a little too short. I had no hair on my face, typically wore khaki pants, and looked like I was about sixteen years old.

When I went outside to grab a quick lunch, from time to time I would run into Andre, who was pushing his drugs and wearing flashy jewelry and the latest clothes.

"I'm working down at city council, man," I once related proudly.

Andre, who rarely traveled anywhere without at least one or two henchmen trailing him, looked at me with disdain.

"Hey, Scoey, you need a couple of dollars, man?" he would say, then laugh sarcastically. Every time he smirked, every time he got in one of his little asshole digs, that just motivated me a little more.

As my arrangement with Bowman began to wind down, I hoped that the council president would take me on full time afterward. But just in case, I was networking at a frantic pace around the council, trying to present myself as best I could.

One of my frequent stops was in the city council's legal research office, where there was a deputy director named Barbara Roper. She had a caring air that reminded me of my mother. A week or two before my informal internship ended, she let me know there would be a position open in her office, but warned that it would be for very low pay.

I got the impression she pulled strings to create that slot for me, which carried the title of special projects assistant. I think it might have paid like five bucks an hour and I began working that job in February 1983.

A month earlier I had begun taking two more graduate-level courses at Eastern Michigan, and I was riding the Greyhound between Ypsilanti and Detroit five days a week, depending on a cheap brown overcoat to ward off the brutal Michigan winter. I soon tired of depending on the gray dog for my transportation and purchased an eight-year-old brown Chevrolet Monte Carlo for about two thousand dollars.

That Monte Carlo made life tremendously easier, lemme tell you.

At some point during the winter of 1983 it came to my attention that Jesse Jackson was considering making a run for president. The woman running Jackson's Detroit campaign was none other than Annette Rainwater, whom I had met at the Operation Push forum with the Reverend Jackson.

Rainwater was the top assistant to city councilman Clyde Cleveland and was trying to assist me as I went around City Hall in an effort to find a full-time job.

Well aware of the historical significance of what Jesse was trying to do, I started volunteering on his campaign. I did gofer work, stuffing envelopes and the like. He was scheduled to come to Detroit and I was thrilled to have the opportunity to see him again.

After a while, I started hearing scuttlebutt that Mrs. Roper's boss, who was very conservative, wasn't a big fan of mine. I was told that she wasn't thrilled to hear that I backed Jesse and Louis Farrakhan, so it was starting to look as though I might have to find another job.

When Jesse came to town for his rally at the Little Rock Baptist Church, I got in his face. Not only did he not remember me, he acted like he wasn't even listening to me, to be honest. I would talk to him and he would just keep looking straight ahead. He's like that to this day and I still find that habit a little insulting.

After acting as though he didn't hear a word I said inside the Little Rock Baptist Church, Jesse eventually walked over to Rainwater, pointed at me, and said: "Make this young man the youth director for the state. It seems like he has some energy that we could use."

Rainwater responded with some smart-mouth comment, which is her way. She gets away with that because when she's involved in a campaign, Rainwater does an awesome job of generating grassroots interest.

At that same rally for Jesse, I met Farrakhan, who was always surrounded by at least ten bow tie–wearing Fruit of Islam bodyguards. His people were talking about him like he was a divine human being instead of a mere mortal.

When the doors of the church opened to the public, it was my first encounter with the crème de la crème of Detroit's black consciousness movement. The current mayor, Coleman Young, was not supporting Jesse Jackson and was backing Walter Mondale instead.

Farrakhan and Jesse came to the church together in a limo, with about fifty Fruit of Islam creating a corridor from the church to the limo, standing stiff and strong like soldiers. Farrakhan had donated his Fruit of Islam security detail, as well as his time, to back Jesse's presidential bid.

Farrakhan spoke for nearly an hour. It was perhaps the most dynamic and powerful speech I had heard since listening to Jesse in 1977. Farrakhan spoke of black economic and political empowerment and black unity. I became an instant Farrakhan admirer.

Then Jesse Jackson ascended to the pulpit. The huge crowd inside the church chanted, "Run, Jesse, run." I was absolutely transfixed by what I was watching, because I had never seen anything like it in my life.

I said to myself, "This is what I want to do." There was so much power and so much impressive black manhood present that night. Louis Farrakhan and Jesse Jackson reminded me so much of street guys who didn't take no stuff and who demanded their props.

It was almost as though the unspoken message was, White America, these are real men, and this is what real men do.

When I returned to work the following Monday, I talked about Farrakhan and Jackson to everybody who would listen. I also got a piece of fantastic news that day, because Rainwater persuaded Councilman Clyde Cleveland to hire me for his staff, so I would be working with him and Rainwater from that point forward. For six dollars an hour, too, instead of the five bucks I had been making.

Cleveland required me to answer letters from constituents regarding their concerns about city government. In addition, I would be going to meetings with Rainwater and taking care of campaign stuff for Jesse.

So now I'm working under the wing of Annette Rainwater, but little did I know that the experience would turn out to be a huge baptism by fire. She cursed me out at least five times every damn day, made me feel like I was stupid, naïve, and born yesterday.

She pushed everything about me, including my endurance level and my skills, to the very limit. But I could feel the love behind what she was doing and always saw that her focus was solely on advancing our projects, or enhancing my professional development.

I used to cringe at the thought of walking into work in the morning, but I was growing and learning at a tremendous pace.

I had taken the Law School Admission Test at Eastern Michigan University and had generated a score that was okay but didn't indicate I might be a budding Thurgood Marshall. Combine that with a 2.5 GPA generated during my undergraduate years and you don't come up with a combination that wows Harvard Law School or Yale Law School.

So when I began to apply to law school in the spring of 1983, I approached it realistically. No sense wasting application fees on the top-tier law schools in the country, because I knew that the odds were slim to none of my being admitted.

Consequently, I applied to thirty law schools that either had middle-of-the-road reputations or aggressive affirmative action programs. Once my applications were out, I waited anxiously for my target schools to start responding. None of them said a word in April. They were still quiet in May, and the silence had grown deafening by June.

Rainwater and Linda would ask me periodically if I had heard anything and I had developed a stock answer to that query: "No, but I'm sure I'll hear something soon." Beneath that show of confidence, however, I was quietly dying. In addition to my mediocre grades and average LSAT score, I had a criminal record.

It wasn't possible to get rejected by thirty out of thirty law schools, was it?

The drought finally ended in July when the University of Mississippi School of Law said, Come on down, y'all. I was deliriously happy to get their letter and was prepared to develop a taste for mint juleps by the fall if necessary.

My second acceptance letter came from the University of Oregon, before the University of Detroit chimed in with a yes. It was right down the street from City Hall, which would allow me to remain employed, would keep me near Linda, and would let me keep my hand in Detroit politics.

The University of Detroit made its acceptance conditional on my being able to complete a five-week summer program, but I had no problem with that provision. I enrolled in the summer program, which consisted only of a criminal law course in which I had to earn at least a C average.

Rainwater and Cleveland both gave me their blessings and were very supportive. Rainwater also ratcheted down the work I had to do with the Jackson campaign.

If you know anything about me by now, it's that I have a tendency to take the rockiest path imaginable. So in addition to working at City Hall and on the Jackson campaign and going to the law school program, I signed up to take a summer graduate-level course at Eastern Michigan, calling for me to maintain a B average.

Twenty-three other black students were enrolled in the University of Detroit Law School summer program, and they were an interesting mix of bourgeois, down-to-earth, and streetwise. We had a black law professor named David Williams who looked to be in his mid-thirties and was very helpful and accessible.

My initial impression of that summer law school program was that it was going to be easy. Once it started, it became apparent to me the degree to which my rights and the rights of other poor people are consistently violated. We read case after case in which individuals and corporations with cash were able to get Lady Justice to do whatever they wanted. Like everything else in this country, the judicial system is skewed in favor of the wealthy.

Professor Williams wasted little time sharing a take on law school that made a lot of sense to me. He said that if we applied ourselves then we should be able to make it through law school with little problem, because it wasn't nearly as difficult or mysterious as the establishment made it appear. Professor Williams told us that if we put in the time to do the reading and writing law school called for, we could make it.

When the five-week program was almost over, the only thing left to do was take a test. Like finals for law school courses, it would be the only test we would have during the entire five-week program. It would determine whether we got into the University of Detroit School of Law or crashed and burned.

I took three days off from work to study for that flippin' test and got only a few hours of sleep the night before it was given. I allowed that examination to get to me, because I was aware that if I failed I had already passed on opportunities to attend two other law schools.

Succumbing to defeatist thinking, I began to devise alternatives to practicing law, before catching myself.

"Why are you thinking like this, Greg? You've never failed at *any-thing* you've tried! What makes you think you're gonna start now?"

When the day of the exam came, I looked around the classroom at the other students waiting to take it, the expression on my face one of cool indifference to the test and everything law school stood for. Rest assured that just behind that nonchalant facade I was shitting bricks.

Professor Williams passed out twenty-four small answer booklets. There was an area on the front of the book to write my name, date, and the class I was being tested for. I would come to dread the sight of those little blue answer booklets.

Then the test questions were placed facedown on our desks as Professor Williams silently glided past each student like an academic Grim Reaper. Taking my watch off my left wrist, I laid it atop my desk in order to keep track of time.

"You have ninety minutes to complete this test," Professor Williams said. "Just relax, apply what we've talked about, and you shouldn't have any problem. Okay, begin now." The classroom was immediately filled with the sound of rustling test question sheets. My moment of truth was upon me.

My test-taking techniques weren't terribly refined, so I glanced at all six questions on the test, clogging up my head with unnecessary information, instead of concentrating on the first question. Noticing that question number four was something I was totally unprepared to write about, I immediately flew into a funk. So much so that when I set out to deal with the first question, I was still thinking about question number four. Come on, don't worry about that now, I told myself. Five out of six should still allow you to ace this thing!

I threw myself into dealing with the first question and answered it thoroughly, but took about twenty-five minutes to finish. That meant I would have to rush through the other questions, because we had been given fifteen minutes for each question.

What was that rule we learned in class for dealing with legal questions? That's right—issue, rule, analysis, conclusion. IRAC. I used IRAC to slog my way through the next two questions before I got to the fourth question. By this time, people are getting up and handing in their tests, looking smug or relieved. Oh shit!

Feeling panic begin to overtake me, I started to pray. Hard.

Dear God, please help me here. Lord, I'm trying to do what you want me to do. You don't want me to go back to the streets, do you? I won't have any choice but to join Andre and them.

With that, I went back to grappling with the test as best I could, until Professor Williams's voice rang out, "Time's up!" I wasn't quite finished, but I took a good run at all of the questions, with the exception of number four. I had only written a few sentences for that one, and they were mostly bullshit.

The exam was administered on a Thursday, and I wouldn't know until Monday if I had passed. When I called the University of Detroit School of Law's admissions office Monday morning and asked if the test scores had been posted, they weren't up yet.

The fourth time I called the grades had finally been placed on a hallway bulletin board in the law school, so I jumped up from my desk in Clyde Cleveland's office in City Hall and jogged about four blocks to the law school, never once breaking stride.

I breezed directly to the bulletin board and quickly located the test score that corresponded to the anonymous number I had been assigned. I had earned an 82 out of a possible 100. Thank you, thank you, thank you Lord Jesus!

Other students were also gazing at their test scores and I didn't want to flaunt my success in case someone hadn't done well, but I couldn't resist pumping my fist in the air at least once.

I had an intoxicating sense of having beaten the system once again.

I had harbored serious doubts as to whether I belonged in law school, based on my background. Most law students came from lives of such privilege that I felt I had defied daunting odds to join them in such a prestigious setting.

"I done got 'em again, Mama," I muttered happily under my breath. "I know I'm not supposed to be in this place, but here we are!"

I was officially enrolled in the University of Detroit School of Law's night program, which caters primarily to working students and requires four years to graduate. The day students, on the other hand, were professional students and took a more concentrated course load that allowed them to graduate in three years. Those who earn the best grades get lucrative job offers from the nation's top law firms. Even though I was pretty certain I was headed toward a career in politics and civil rights, I still wanted to have the option of working with a high-paying firm should I decide on a career change.

With this objective in mind, I promised myself I wouldn't miss a single class during my first semester in law school. That would take a little doing, since I was working full-time, was helping out with Jesse Jackson's presidential campaign in Detroit, and would be taking three classes my initial semester. The subjects I would be studying were torts, property, and contracts.

Not long after I was admitted to the University of Detroit School of Law, I ran into Andre at a nightclub. I couldn't wait to tell him what I was doing, but true to form he downplayed it.

"Good," he said with an insincere smile. "Maybe I'll hire you. Maybe you can be my consigliere." Then he pulled out a wad of bills thick as a tree trunk and offered to buy me a drink.

It wouldn't have made any difference if I had told Andre I was about to become CEO of the Ford Motor Company, because he would have belittled that, too.

On the first day of law school I arrived in the suit that I had worn to work that day. As I looked around our classroom to see who had survived from my summer class, I was surprised by the size of my class, which was approximately 120 students. The class makeup was overwhelmingly white, with about twenty African Americans mixed in. Most of the budding lawyers present appeared to be in their late twenties or early thirties. My first professor wasted little time spouting what would soon become a tired intimidation tactic: "First of all, I want all of you to look at the student to your left," he said, and we obediently followed his instruction. "Now look at the student to your right. One of them is not going to make it through law school."

That was an immediate turnoff, in light of the nurturing, supportive atmosphere Professor Williams had fostered during the summer program. However, far from being nervous or anxious about my ability to make it through law school, I was feeling confident. I had applied myself during Professor Williams's class and had received an 82. Therefore, there was no reason to think I would graduate with less than a B average.

If you've never attended law school, it doesn't typically attract folks who are lacking in self-confidence or who have a burning desire to be a team player. It didn't take long for me to see I was surrounded primarily by insufferable know-it-alls, arrogant people who were so ridiculously competitive that they would deliberately misfile resource materials in the law library so no one else could use them.

Instead of being put off by that, I decided to turn it up a notch against those privileged folks whose educational opportunities and lives in general had given them a leg up on me.

If anything, I felt like I had an advantage over them, because they hadn't overcome as many obstacles in life as I had. So I felt I was more resourceful and more determined. In the first few weeks I fell in with a group of five black students who formed a loosely organized study group. We had an unspoken agreement not to get caught up in the madness that typifies law school.

Something that amazed me right off the bat was the incredible load of cases we had to read to prepare for classes. There were literally hundreds of pages of textbook and supplementary material that had to be pored over each night.

Fortunately, everybody at my job was supportive of my law-degree quest. As long as I met my responsibilities, I could prop my books up in my cubicle and read them openly.

One person who definitely had my back when I started law school was Linda. She was still at Eastern Michigan, which was a good thing. Due to the incredible demands that legal education makes on your time and energy, there was a saying that if you were married, law school would become your mistress, and if you weren't married, law school would become your spouse.

I was initially skeptical about that, but toward the beginning of my first semester I saw it was definitely true.

One class I developed an intense dislike for was contracts, because it was taught by a nightmarish professor who loved to lord it over students and bedazzle us with his incredible brilliance. Hell, if I taught the same course over and over again, I'd probably come off as incredibly brilliant, too.

Everybody was terrified to be called on to answer a question in contracts class, because the professor explained things in such an esoteric way that it was very hard to grasp what the hell he was talking about. I was sitting in contracts one day around the second or third week of class when the professor asked one of his obtuse, ultracomplicated questions.

Naturally no one volunteered to answer, so this professor ran a finger down his enrollment sheet and bellowed, "Greg Mathis!"

I showed no reaction whatsoever and just kept staring straight ahead, waiting for that fool to call somebody else. I figured he didn't know me from Adam's housecat, so why should I step forward to be publicly humiliated?

The professor paused about fifteen seconds, frowning as he stared at his enrollment sheet. Then he again cried out: "Greg Mathis!" This time, several of the black kids I had gone through the summer program with swiveled in their seats and began staring directly at me!

I turned around, too, looking to see if this Greg Mathis character was sitting behind me or something.

Despite the fact that I attended every class and studied really hard,

I had two Cs and a B when my grades came back. That was a disillusioning experience, because it only seems fair that if you fully extend yourself in pursuit of a goal, you should get back a stellar result.

It was clear that I was not going to be on the A list for any silk-stocking law firm. But that doesn't make any difference, I rationalized. God didn't bring me this far just to be some rich, high-powered attorney anyway.

During the next semester, instead of behaving like a drone that ate, breathed, and slept the law, I decided it would be better to divide my focus between law school and my career. So instead of slavishly showing up for class each and every night, I began picking and choosing which nights to attend. I missed maybe 10 percent of my classes.

The Jackson campaign had also started to heat up in January 1984, calling for me to devote more time and attention to it. I had given law school 150 percent during my first semester and felt that the grades I had received hadn't matched the effort I had put in. So now I was only giving part of myself to law school and reserving the rest for my real passion, which was politics.

It tickled me to death to show up for class wearing "Jackson for President" buttons, because that invariably caused consternation among some of my classmates. Good. They never had the courage to say anything to my face, so to hell with 'em.

After giving law school only part of my focus I still got Cs and Bs after the second semester, just as I had when I busted my ass during the first semester. That helped me to determine my attendance pattern and exertion level for the rest of my law school tenure.

Rainwater and I had been working hard in the Detroit area to help Jesse Jackson beat Walter Mondale in the Democratic presidential primary. Even so, Mondale won, thanks in part to the fact that Detroit mayor Coleman Young had put his impressive political machine behind Mondale.

I had been taking classes nonstop since 1978, first at Eastern Michigan University, now at the University of Detroit School of Law. I may have had an undeniable thirst for education, but I needed a damn break from classrooms. So I didn't take any summer courses during the summer of 1984.

When August arrived and classes started back up again, instead of skipping 10 percent of them as I had the previous semester, I blew off 20 percent. Which was just as well, because I got tired of listening to many of my classmates gloat after Ronald Reagan trounced Walter Mondale for the presidency in November.

I took my final exams in December and the same grades came back as always—Cs and Bs. I was starting to wonder if I could blow off 90 percent of my classes, study hard for final exams, and still get the same result.

After several years of living with my oldest brother, Ron, I moved out of his nice neighborhood on the city's East Side and got a studio apartment on the West Side that was about ten minutes away from Herman Gardens.

I was eating an awful lot of Hamburger Helper in those days, so I definitely looked forward to Linda's weekend visits when she came from Eastern Michigan.

After I moved from his place, Ron cosigned for me to get a decent late-model white Pontiac coupe. So I was pleased with where I was in life. I wasn't making lightning-fast progress, but I was moving forward.

I was slowly moving away from the instant gratification mind-set that blocks the development of so many young African Americans.

Which brings me to my boy Andre, who had become the poster boy for those who gotta have the good life *right now* and who think sacrifice and long-range planning are for squares.

I ran up on him on one occasion when I was about to enter a club with a childhood buddy who was a mutual friend. A master of grand entrances, Andre arrived on the scene in a cherry red drop-top BMW, trailed by a car loaded with his sycophants.

Andre and his boys were draped in what had to be tens of thousands of dollars' worth of gaudy jewelry. With his entourage stretching behind him like obedient black ducklings, Andre rolled up in the club looking like a black mafia godfather.

"What's up, Scoey?" he said, shooting me a sharklike grin at the front door. "Lemme buy you some champagne." Of course, that meant purchasing not a glass, but a bottle of the most expensive stuff behind the bar. In the meantime, I waited for the insult or disparaging remark that I knew was coming. For some reason, Andre took malicious delight in flashing on me.

"So what's up, man—you getting any money yet?" Andre said casually, as his entourage listened attentively.

"Naw, Andre, I ain't gettin' rich yet. But I'm doing important work."

"Yeah, I hear you've been chasing Jesse Jackson around town, holding his dick," he said as his boys dissolved into raucous laughter. "You gettin' any money off that?"

"No, I'm just paying my dues," I responded sheepishly. I was seething inwardly, but I damn sure didn't want him to have the satisfaction of knowing.

When the waitress arrived, Andre resorted to his usual routine of pulling out a thick wad of hundred-dollar bills, pretty much making a mockery of what I was doing. Then he sailed off to a different part of the club to do his thing.

I hung around with my buddy for a few more minutes, feeling totally and thoroughly humiliated. And I felt determined, too, determined that at some point I was going to show Andre I had taken the right path.

My feelings about Andre had grown terribly conflicted. On the one hand, he had become a brother with whom I carried out the most intense sibling rivalry imaginable. I was burning to show him I was just as talented as he was and ultimately was going to be more successful. A helluva lot more successful.

But there was also a part of me that despised Andre, because I felt he was causing a lot of death and destruction to black people through his drug dealing. And I thought he either didn't care about that or was too blinded by his self-importance to recognize it.

He may have had BMWs and showy jewelry, but in my opinion I was the successful one. I had a bachelor's degree, I was in law school, and I was associating with the mayor and national leaders like Louis Farrakhan and Jesse Jackson.

Andre might be sipping Dom Perignon and flashing massive bankrolls of blood money, but I still believed my way was the right way. I had seen hundreds of hustlers like Andre go down in flames, and I knew that it was only a matter of time before his turn came, too.

When December 1984 rolled around, I had another momentous decision to make. Linda was going to graduate in May, and I knew there were certain unspoken expectations on her part.

In my mind there was a silent understanding that once Linda graduated from college the two of us would get married. We knew after four and a half years together that we wanted to be partners for the rest of our lives. But to Linda's everlasting credit, I never received any pressure from her.

I loved the way her parents had always been totally supportive and accepting of me, despite my rough edges. That really endeared me to the family, because most middle-class blacks thought I was way beneath them.

Now I was facing a question. How long could I hold on to Linda in our unmarried state before she eventually drifted away?

Knowing that I wanted to have a family with her, I figured there was no time like the present to deal with the issue. I had a plan, and we spent Christmas Eve at her parents' suburban Detroit home to put the wheels in motion.

On Christmas morning I woke up and escorted Linda to a beautifully decorated fir tree in the living room. Among the many gifts under the tree was a huge red-and-silver box that appeared to contain a television set.

When I told Linda it was for her, she looked a little disappointed. Only the two of us were in the family room as Linda started attacking that box, in which I had put some old shoes to give it some weight.

First she ripped off the gift wrapping, looking perplexed, because I was acting as though there was an extraordinary gift inside. Once the outer wrapping was gone, a cardboard box for a television unit appeared under the Christmas tree.

"Oh, a television," Linda said quietly, looking extremely disappointed. It was all I could do not to bust out laughing. "Why is the box already open, Greg?"

A comical shrug was my only response.

"All right, then," Linda said, suddenly interested again. "Let's see what's up." She pulled back a flap on the box and was surprised to see newspaper and balled-up pieces of wrapping paper inside. She started beaming immediately, her expression growing more radiant by the second.

When all the wrapping paper and newspaper had been flung onto the floor, Linda spied a jet black ring case at the bottom of the box with a huge smile. The ring case held a quarter-carat diamond engagement ring I had dropped about seven hundred dollars on.

"Oh Greg, thank you," Linda exclaimed loudly, and immediately kissed me. I still hadn't said anything by that point, so Linda kissed me again, a long hard smooch that suddenly had me wishing we were alone, instead of at her parents' place.

When our lips separated, I looked Linda right in the eye and said: "Well? Will you?" I just couldn't form my mouth to say "Will you marry me?" because it seemed so corny and clichéd.

"Yes!" Linda quickly squealed, kissing me again. Then she started screaming, awakening her parents. They wandering into the living room wearing their pajamas and knowing smiles.

"What's the deal?"

When they found out, both of them hugged me, and Linda's

mother kissed me on the cheek. Her parents asked me for a date when we planned to jump the broom, and I suggested early June.

Linda was delighted to hear that, not knowing if I might try to string things out another year or two before actually taking that walk down the aisle. But well before any of that could take place, I had an admission to make to Linda that could potentially change her mind about marriage.

I usually only saw Linda on weekends after she drove from Eastern Michigan University, and the sisters who worked at City Hall were well aware of that. I had been very good at skirting temptation for the most part, but about six months before I proposed to Linda I encountered a City Hall coworker who definitely caught my eye.

My job called for me to walk to an office where this woman worked as a clerk. She was seven years my senior, making her thirty-one, and she was pretty. She was flirtatious and I flirted right back.

My smiling and grinning was with the hope of one day seeing my friend's pretty black hair cascading across a pair of beautiful brown nipples. I ain't gonna lie.

After a number of weeks of flirting and steadily rising sexual tension, she invited me to accompany her to her church! Unsure of whether she was merely inviting me to church or inviting me on a date, I rationalized in my mind that I wouldn't be cheating on Linda by going to church with this woman. So I agree to attend an evening service at my coworker's place of worship.

When I drove by her house to pick her up, she appeared wearing a long dress that flowed down to her ankles.

Am I cheating on Linda just by being with this woman? I thought. Do I even want to cheat on Linda? Am I feeling lust here or love?

The entire time we rode to my coworker's church we didn't talk about anything outside of work or about how enthralled she was by the Christian fellowship we would be experiencing shortly.

Even though I wasn't impressed with her church in the least, I pretended to really like it so I could be invited back. The pastor was just some charlatan faith healer who had people come down in front in wheelchairs, then they would miraculously hop up after being healed. People who had walked into the church leaning heavily on canes threw them aside and ran up the church aisle like Olympic track stars. Please!

I immediately saw this to be the fake-ass shit that it was. Sometime later the pastor in charge of the church was convicted of narcotics possession and subsequently had a nervous breakdown, but that didn't prevent me from going back to his church a second time with my coworker, primarily because I had begun to view her as a sexual challenge. My old doggish ways were returning—after wrestling back and forth with the thought of cheating on Linda, I concluded that I would.

So I picked up my coworker for a second time and endured more of that church nonsense she found so fascinating. But after the service, this time I asked her to stop by my brother Steve's house with me. I had an apartment of my own, but Linda had a bad habit of sometimes popping up there unexpectedly. So I gave Steve my car keys and told him to get lost. Then I took my coworker back into a spare bedroom.

After we finished making love, we immediately regretted what we had done. She allowed that passion had gotten the better of her because she hadn't been with a man for more than a year.

I admitted that our little liaison wasn't the best move I could have possibly made, either, because I was involved in a relationship with someone that I cared deeply about. So we parted company that night agreeing to be friends and nothing else.

That one time we connected was it—we never got together again. I avoided her for a couple of weeks afterward, because frankly I was embarrassed that my canine side had gotten the better of me.

My coworker called me once and I didn't even return her call. When I finally did, six weeks later, she said something that turned my young world on its ear: "I'm pregnant, Greg!"

"What!" I yelled out in Councilman Clyde Cleveland's office as my heart began fluttering like mad. "Oh shit—we're gonna have to talk this over! How could that have happened?"

As soon as I hung up the phone, I started muttering under my breath. "Shit—what the fuck! Linda is going to kill my ass!"

I began to think immediately of my relationship with Linda coming to an end over this. I simply could not allow that to happen.

My coworker and I met for lunch at a downtown restaurant. She had a serious look on her face as she glanced into my eyes from time to time. I'm sure I looked panicky and nervous enough to jump out of my skin.

"How have you been feeling?" I asked, trying to act sensitive and concerned.

I picked at my food during that lunch, which was without question the quietest, most solemn one I have ever had. I didn't bring up the fact that my coworker was pregnant and neither did she. It wasn't until I got back in my car that I broached the subject.

As casually as I could possibly manage, I turned to her and said, "What are we going to do?"

I immediately began racking my brain for ways to explain my dilemma to Linda. And I wondered again if she and I could survive this.

Following our luncheon date, I was distant from my coworker, mainly because I wasn't 100 percent certain the baby she was carrying was mine, but I didn't want to insult her.

She had full health insurance, and I didn't really think that she would need me for anything up to the day that she delivered her baby. I didn't feel an obligation to spend any time with her during her pregnancy, and she didn't ask me to.

We never told anyone around City Hall that I was the father of her child. Throughout her pregnancy, I would go into her office on routine business, which was my way of touching base with her and making sure everything was all right.

I think she understood my situation with Linda, whom I had proposed to while knowing full well that my friend was pregnant.

A couple of months after accepting my marriage offer, Linda was happily making wedding plans and anticipating her upcoming graduation from Eastern Michigan University in a few months. There was little question this was one of the happiest periods in my fiancée's life. But now, because I had let my little head think for me, I had to ruin things with a big load of unhappiness and heartbreak. I must have avoided bringing up the subject on at least twenty occasions.

But I finally screwed up my courage and invited Linda to join me for dinner at one of Detroit's most exclusive steakhouses.

We went there dressed to the nines, with Linda excitedly looking forward to a memorable, incredibly romantic evening. Little did she know that I was shaking like a damn leaf as we entered that restaurant and took our seats. Because I was still wavering even at that point, not sure if I was going to tell her that night or not. That may seem cowardly, unless you've ever had to drop that kind of devastating news on someone in that situation.

There was a little piano bar in the restaurant and as we grooved to the music and enjoyed our food, Linda merrily jabbered away about the wedding and about her plans for the future.

When she paused for a second, I took a really, really deep breath.

"Linda, is there anything that could possibly happen at this point that could stop this?" I asked, taking pains to keep a quaver out of my voice. "I sure hope nothing could keep us from getting married." Not surprisingly, Linda looked at me oddly.

"What in the world are you talking about, Greg?" she asked in a strange voice as her pretty hazel eyes probed my face like twin lasers. "We're about to be married and I hope *nothing* derails this. Are you getting cold feet or something?"

"No, baby, I definitely ain't getting cold feet. There's no question in my mind that you're the woman I want to spend the rest of my life with . . . but sometimes things happen that can fuck everything up," I said. "Sometimes couples get into arguments and fall out while they're engaged. Old lovers might show up and sometimes people make mistakes that come back to haunt them."

By then Linda was looking at me like I was going crazy. She wasn't that far off the mark, either.

"Greg, what are you talking about?"

I gulped, knowing that it was time to stop tap dancing. "Is there any mistake that either of us could make that would cause us to cancel this wedding?"

"No," she answered instantly, to my relief. "There's nothing either party could do to derail these wedding plans."

"Well, I'm glad to hear that, because I made a mistake," I said, straining to get the words out of my throat.

"What? What have you done, Greg?"

"While you were up at Eastern Michigan it was hard on me down here, Linda. And I slipped up and had a one-night stand." Linda looked relieved to hear that, but her relief would prove short-lived. "And now, the woman is pregnant." As difficult as that was to say, it took a heavy weight off my shoulders to do it.

Linda looked at me in disbelief, then slowly lowered her head into her hands. Without seeing her face, I could tell she was crying. "We can leave, Greg," Linda said in a barely audible voice.

I jumped up immediately and walked Linda outside to my car, then came back into the restaurant to pay the bill. Then I came back outside and began driving the love of my life back to her parents' house. Not having the foggiest idea what to say, I remained silent.

"Who is the woman?" Linda said finally. "And where did you meet her?"

"I have to go to the woman's office to get checks for city council employees," I said, trying to sound pitiful. "I really wasn't paying any attention to her, but she kept telling me that no man should be without a spiritual anchor and that I should go to her church one evening."

"Some sisters are desperate for professional men," Linda suddenly spat out venomously, fighting mad. Her anger wasn't directed at me, so I took that as a good sign.

"One day we just stopped by Steve's, because he ain't too far from her church," I continued, glancing over at Linda in case she might consider popping me in the head or something. "And when we got over there, she seduced me. You can even ask Steve."

"How many times were you with this woman?" Linda asked in a clipped voice.

"It only happened one time," I said, glad that for once I didn't have to embellish the truth.

"You sure it was only one time?"

I reassured Linda that I had been pure as the driven snow before and after that one encounter.

Linda didn't say much else as the sights of downtown Detroit glided past my car windows. I could tell that she was still struggling to process the information that I was fathering a child outside our relationship. I didn't blame her at all.

"Baby, don't let nothin' destroy our plans, because we have a great life in front of us," I said.

To Linda's credit, she never brought up the baby again after that night. She acted as if it didn't even exist, so I took my cue from her and kept my mouth shut. But I knew it would reenter our lives, because I wasn't going to put blinders on and make believe I had no responsibilities outside of my marriage.

I didn't mention my love child again, until months and months later. I was headed out one night and Linda was insisting on knowing where I was disappearing to.

"If you must know, the woman had the baby. And I'm going to see the baby."

"Oh, she had it?" Linda said, grimacing. "What was it, a girl or a boy?"

"It was a girl, and her name is Jade."

"Hmpphh!"

The entire episode demonstrated to me that Linda is a model of tolerance, which made me love her even more. My baby showed her that I still had some growing to do in regard to my manhood and sexuality, and she was willing to help me with that. Since that time Jade has been an equal member of my family along with my other children and continues to spend many holidays and weekends with us.

Linda graduated from Eastern Michigan University with a degree in early childhood development in May 1985. When she walked across that stage, I felt prouder of her than I did of myself when I got out of Eastern Michigan.

Through my City Council ties, I had come to know a Detroit school board member named Alonzo Bates. Alonzo made it possible for Linda to get a position as director of preschool activities within Detroit's public schools system.

Not only were my political connections starting to pay off, but they even managed to earn me some brownie points with my fiancée. And Lord knew that I needed them.

On the last day of May, a bunch of my old boys from the 'hood threw a bachelor party for me at my place. By that time I had moved into the apartment I planned to share with my wife-to-be, in a high-rise near downtown Detroit. A bunch of strippers sashayed all over my place while the boys and I drank liquor and had a good ol' time.

The following day, June 1, 1985, was a beautiful Saturday with perfect weather. It was storming inside my head though, because all the oil my crew and I had consumed the night before had me hung over. So my first order of business on my wedding day was to knock back a couple of pain relievers.

A buddy who owned a Mercedes sedan came by to pick up me and my best man, Craig Lewis, who was a friend from my Herman Gardens days. We had a twenty-minute ride to the Temple of Faith Baptist Church, on the West Side of Detroit and not far from where I grew up.

I was one nervous, hyper brother as that Mercedes rolled toward Faith Baptist. My mind was whirling at the speed of light, mulling over the huge step I was about to take.

I needed Linda's stabilizing influence in my life and I wanted and needed to have a family of my own. And Linda was the woman I wanted to do it with. Yet I still was edgy.

When we arrived at the church, I immediately became aware that everyone was checking me out to see how I looked and how I was handling things. Which of course kicked my nervousness into overdrive. Craig and my boys noticed this too, because they immediately started ragging on me once we got inside the church, where three hundred people waited.

When I walked down the center church aisle to await the arrival of the bride, I put on this big smile that belied my jittery inner state. When Linda came gliding down toward me on her father's arm, I had to fight back the tears. One of my brothers, Steve, sang at my wedding, and I felt Mama's presence that day, without question.

Something else that sticks in my mind about my wedding was the sight of Andre and two of his goons decked out in the most expensive jewelry imaginable loitering outside the church. He looked every inch the infamous, high-rolling drug dealer that he was.

"Whassup, Scoey?" he yelled out from a distance, smirking as usual and not even bothering to congratulate me.

"Thanks for coming, Andre," I shouted back.

Linda and I climbed into my buddy's Mercedes and headed for a downtown hotel where the reception was taking place. I have to take my hat off to Linda's father, because he dropped some big cheese—fifteen grand—on our wedding.

The following morning, my new wife and I jetted off to Ocho Rios, Jamaica. We spent a few magical days at a villa atop a cliff that afforded us a magnificent view of the Caribbean Sea.

X

BURYING HOMEBOYS

I returned from my honeymoon to the devastating news that my friend Vincent had been killed in a crack house in Detroit. My relaxed state after being in the Caribbean hadn't even worn off before I was reintroduced to the gritty, stark reality of inner-city life.

Vince and two other men were in the crack house allegedly selling drugs when someone stormed in and gunned them down. One of the men lived, but my homeboy and the other man didn't make it.

Like me, Vince had been born and raised in the Seventh-Day Adventist Church, and had attended Peterson Academy along with Andre, Rick, and me. Vince and I used to spend the night together as kids, and we had been very close friends most of our lives.

I had advised Vince not to join Andre in the heroin trade, but he had a mind of his own. Vince's funeral was held in the same Seventh-Day Adventist church where he, Andre, and I had grown up.

Andre remained outside with his clownish jewelry, fancy clothes, and red BMW convertible, just as he had at my wedding.

Inside the church, Vince's body lay inside a closed casket, because he had been so badly riddled by bullets.

Why did Andre have him involved in the deadly narcotics trade when he knew Vince really wasn't up to that game?

I was a pallbearer at Vince's funeral, and when I helped bring his casket outside, Andre was standing near the church steps with his head bowed. I tried to see if he had any pain in his face, because I was in such incredible pain myself. I wanted to see if he was so cold-blooded that now nothing affected him. What I saw was an expression that conveyed sadness and shame. That let me know that Andre still had a bit of a heart left, that apparently a human was still tucked away in his body somewhere. Many of those who had attended the funeral weren't so certain, judging from the biting remarks they uttered under their breath and the contemptuous looks shot in Andre's direction.

That same summer, another lifelong friend died of a drug overdose. Alonzo Fears had dropped out of school in his teens and had become engulfed in the street life, primarily to support a lifelong drug and alcohol habit.

Once again I found myself serving as a pallbearer for a dear, departed friend.

While I was at Alonzo's funeral, I found myself rehashing a lot of our history. I recalled how the first time I had gotten into trouble, it had been with Alonzo. We had been troubled kids together, and when I began to overcome my difficulties, I continued to come back to Prairie Street four or five times a year to see Alonzo. He was still my friend, and we never passed judgment on each other and still loved each other, even though he was going down a self-destructive path. All my attempts to nudge him in the right direction had failed, and that really bothered me.

The statistics I heard in 1985 about black youths dying were hitting home in a very personal way. I started thinking, Hey, I work at City Hall—isn't there something I can do to stop this carnage? Am I doing everything that I possibly can to eliminate the conditions causing so much destruction?

With those questions in mind, I decided to start a self-help youth agency. I spent several months coming up with a plan that would make this pipe-dream agency of mine a reality.

In the spring of 1986, I recruited several buddies who, like me, had managed to extract themselves from the streets and were now moving down the path of self-empowerment. We began to meet on Saturday mornings, planning the debut of an entity that I named Young Adults Asserting Themselves (YAAT).

These three fellas from the 'hood and myself got YAAT under way using just our money. Our plan was to go into impoverished Detroit neighborhoods and hold job and community development workshops inside recreation centers, churches, and community colleges. We hoped this would bring community resources to the people who needed them most.

For motivational speakers, we enlisted the aid of professionals who agreed to serve as role models.

I got permission from the dean of the University of Detroit School of Law to hold our first workshop there. Once we had a venue nailed down, my boys and I distributed approximately five thousand flyers in and around downtown Detroit.

The flyers read: *Wanted! Young adults ages 17 through 28 in search of jobs, training programs, and a college education. Attend a job and career development workshop at the University of Detroit School of Law.* The flyers gave a date for the workshop, but didn't include a contact phone number since there was no staff to answer calls.

That initial workshop took place on a Saturday and about four hundred young people showed up. We ended up having to use three different law school classrooms and had the closing session in the school's atrium.

It wasn't the most well organized or professional of events, given that it represented my first stab at something along those lines. But the important thing was, it was effective. Roughly two hundred participants signed up to visit employment agencies or made appointments to go see community college admissions directors.

I set out to prove those "experts" who claim that black youth don't want to work were wrong, and I succeeded. All that's missing from the lives of hard-core unemployed black youths from the inner city is hope and opportunity. When those two critical ingredients aren't present, poor black kids simply give up on mainstream America and opt instead for a destructive subculture of criminal activity to survive.

Amusingly, the YAAT workshop brought about a rare Greg Mathis sighting at the University of Detroit School of Law. I was only attending law classes about 60 percent of the time now and my grades were slightly lower, having dipped to a typical C as opposed to a B-minus.

I didn't have the kind of grades that would get me a lucrative job as an attorney at one of the country's top law firms. So why kill myself? Instead, I channeled my energy into areas that would allow me to excel in the realms of civil rights and politics.

Professors had begun expressing resentment over my spotty law school attendance and when I did show my face in the place, classmates would feign astonishment and ask, "What are you doing here?"

When I got my grades back after the first semester of my third year in law school, I was convinced that my graders knew who I was, even though the process is supposed to be anonymous. I compared some of the exam answers that had earned me Cs and Ds with similar responses that had gotten some of my classmates As and Bs.

They wanted to play games, huh? Well, I would show them some gamesmanship. I decided that I wouldn't go to classes *at all* during the second semester of my third year in law school. I had two courses and I would show up for the first day of class to get a syllabus and buy the textbooks I needed. But after day one, they could count on not seeing my black ass again until the end of the semester, when it was time to take exams.

So it was that I never appeared for a single lecture, yet still passed both courses with a C and a C-plus. My stunt became legendary and was even more widely talked about than the time the contracts professor called "Greg Mathis!" and I turned around like everyone else.

I had taken a tremendous calculated risk by not going to class like that, but I had a point to prove. I was thumbing my nose at another white institution that I thought wasn't giving me my fair due.

As a result of what I had done, a mandatory attendance policy was immediately implemented within the law school. I had a friend in the registrar's office who told me they were trying to determine if I was technically enrolled in my two courses, because both professors assumed that I had dropped the classes. My gambit caused an uproar and a scandal that sent shock waves all the way to the dean's office. Some of my classmates took to calling the mandatory attendance rule, which said that students could not miss more than four classes without their grades being affected, the Mathis Rule.

People had stopped speaking to me by then, including some of my black classmates. They'd be standing directly in front of me holding a conversation and wouldn't even acknowledge me. I kind of got a kick out of that, frankly.

I was aware that a lot of folks at the law school knew of my troubled background and felt I was flouting a marvelous opportunity that I really didn't deserve in the first place. I guess I was an ungrateful affirmative action baby, judging from the paternalistic, condescending attitudes a lot of people displayed toward me. I took pleasure in showing them I wasn't a "good boy."

My attempt to play the game by the rules, when I had attended each class during my first semester, hadn't yielded results I desired. So I decided to play and succeed based on my own rules. However, what I had ultimately done was cut off my nose to spite my face. One of the students hurt most by the new attendance policy was me! For one thing, I had less latitude to deal with work-related matters and had to reduce my class load from three classes to two. I had a million balls in the air, had no time at all in the evenings after work, and was fatigued all the time.

On top of all this, I was feeling pressure at home in a way that called my manhood into question. Linda was starting to get on my case because she was ready to start a family, but there were no bambinos in sight. She was concerned that something might be wrong and even suggested that I be evaluated by a doctor.

Talk about hitting a brother where he lives! I half-jokingly informed her that I would show her what I could do.

As 1986 drew to a close, everywhere I looked someone was demanding that I step up to the plate and deliver. I was chomping at the bit to prove I was up to the challenge on all fronts.

A few weeks into the New Year, Linda called me at work with "some great news." Even though I suspected, I nearly fell out of my chair when she told me that she was pregnant!

"I told you there was nothing wrong with me," I gloated, laughing. Linda went on to have three children back-to-back until she finally said uncle. With the announcement of each blessed event, naturally I always said, "You still think something is wrong with me? Still want me to go see a doctor?"

In the spring of 1987 I received a phone call from a mutual friend of Andre's and mine. This individual had risen rapidly among the ranks of Detroit's high-rolling drug dealers, which I think made Andre jealous.

Andre had arranged for our friend to join him in a major drug deal. One of Andre's boys delivered a major quantity of cocaine to our friend and collected $32,000 for the product. The problem was that the bag contained nothing but flour. When our friend protested, one of Andre's henchmen stuck a 9-mm handgun in his face. Bilked out of his $32,000, my friend was effectively driven out of business, courtesy of two-timing Andre.

I called up one of Andre's cousins and related what had gone down. "Andre is out of control, man," I told the cousin, whom I trusted and never thought would divulge our conversation. "First he goes and gets Vincent killed, and now this!"

Little did I know that the cousin scurried back to Andre and told him verbatim what I had trustingly uttered.

I found this out one evening while walking from City Hall to one of my law school classes. My path took me past a clothing store called The Broadway, which was one of Andre's favorite hangouts. As I was strolling by, a salesman I knew motioned for me to come inside for a moment.

"Yo man, what's happenin'? I'm about to be late for class here."

"What's up with you and your boy Andre?" the salesman asked, sounding concerned. "I heard you guys have a beef, and he's gonna do a Maserati Rick on you!"

I felt a tingle flow up my spine. Maserati Rick was the name of an infamous city drug dealer who had been gunned down and killed *inside the Broadway*. Andre was crazy and unpredictable enough that I had no choice but to take this secondhand threat at face value.

As a result, I began asking police officers who worked at City Council if I could catch a ride to my car or to law school. I told Linda about Andre's words, which was probably a bad move because she became quite concerned about my safety.

Now that I was officially a square and had relegated the heroic (or foolish) side of my persona to my past, I was kind of worried about me, too. Whenever a kid jogged up behind me on the street, I immediately spun around to see what the hell was up. I avoided the Broadway clothing store, as well as clubs that I knew Andre frequented. And of course I dreaded the sight of red BMW convertibles.

I didn't think Andre would personally cap me, but I didn't doubt he would have one of his boys do a drive-by on me.

One day when I was walking downtown I ran into Andre's father. He was a recently recovered drug addict who was trying to do the right thing and live a decent, productive life. So I talked to him about my feud with Andre and he told me he would intervene. By the summer of 1987 word trickled back from Andre's cousin and others that I just needed to stop talking shit and stay the fuck out of Andre's business. I was told it would be good if Andre's name never escaped my lips, which I had no problem with. It was easy to make believe he didn't even exist.

Not long after that crisis was averted, Jesse Jackson came to Detroit on one of his twice-yearly visits. Rumors were flying that he was considering another run for president on the Democratic ticket, and he confirmed that those rumors were true. In fact, he wanted the folks in his Detroit Operation Push office to establish a Jackson for President committee for the state of Michigan.

This suggestion was made during a meeting at the Little Rock Baptist Church attended by Jesse, Annette Rainwater, Councilman Clyde Cleveland, and myself.

"Okay then," Rainwater said, seated at a table in one of the church's meeting rooms. "I think the person who should run Jesse's Michigan operation happens to be a dynamic young man who's a rising star in Detroit politics. I suggest that Greg Mathis run Michigan for Jesse."

Annette had told me beforehand that she had planned to do that, so I wasn't caught off guard. The same sure couldn't be said of the other fifteen or so folks in that meeting room. A number of them made it quite clear they thought that running Jackson's Michigan presidential campaign was far too awesome a responsibility for me.

I can see why some people may have felt that way. I was twenty-seven and looked twenty-two, with a face that was covered with unimposing peach fuzz instead of thick facial hair. On top of that, I stood six feet tall and probably weighed a buck-fifty. I wasn't what you would call physically imposing, and folks had a habit of looking at me and underestimating me, which I was used to. The important thing was, as I sat at the table wearing my old, cheap suit that was too short in the sleeves, I knew I was up to the task.

The dissenters made their points of view heard, but forceful Annette Rainwater batted down their objections one after another. There was some grumbling, but Annette Rainwater was an influential woman who was used to getting her way. So before that meeting came to an end, her suggestion was law.

Frankly, I didn't think she would be able to pull it off. And when the meeting closed and I was officially Jesse's Michigan coordinator for his upcoming presidential run, I was like, "Oh my God, how am I going to pull this off?"

After the meeting I approached Annette and said, "Mama, you're going to have to help me!"

Then I drove home and told my wife. "Baby, guess who's running Jesse Jackson's presidential campaign in Michigan?"

The position represented the biggest achievement in my life thus far and I had to get rolling on it the very next day. There was no time for preparation or contemplation—I had to get into the mix immediately. Jesse Jackson was someone who had inspired me to lead and to attend college and who had helped shape my adult philosophy on life. Now he was running for president, and I was heading up his campaign in one of the biggest states in the country.

So I took a dramatically reduced load in law school for fall semester 1987. In fact, I arranged to attend classes with the University of Detroit's daytime law students, because I knew that my nights would be tied up.

We began the preparations for the biggest campaign of my life with a series of strategy-setting conference calls between me, state cochair Joel Ferguson—a millionaire member of the Michigan Board of Regents who lived in Lansing—and Annette Rainwater and Clyde Cleveland, who were also state cochairs for Jackson's campaign.

I was well aware that I was in tall grass and I wasn't really sure if I belonged, but my plan was to act as if I did. Ferguson acted as if I were in the way and tried to marginalize me. Rainwater treated me in a maternalistic manner, just as a mother would treat a son. "Do what I say and shut up. I've taught you everything that you know." But Clyde Cleveland treated me as a full partner, for which I was eternally grateful.

The first part of our strategy had to do with getting around the mainstream Democratic political establishment in Michigan, which was firmly in the corner of another Democratic candidate for president, then–Massachusetts governor Michael Dukakis. That meant that the auto unions were behind Dukakis, including the United Auto Workers, the most powerful political force in Michigan.

Locally, Democratic mayor Coleman Young was also a Dukakis

man. Young and the auto workers commanded formidable political machines with hundreds of paid workers at their behest.

On the other hand, Jackson's forces in Michigan were primarily a ragtag web of political activists and volunteers. So our strategy was to first connect with our power base, which was Michigan's African American community. Once that base was solidified, we would spread our influence to other minority groups in pursuit of our Rainbow Coalition.

Along those lines, Detroit has the largest Arab community in the country, as well as a vibrant Latino contingent. We decided to remind the Arabs of how Jackson had always backed the Palestinians' point of view and had made it a point to embrace Yasser Arafat. With the Latinos, we planned to stress that although blacks and Latinos arrived in the States via different routes, we were in the same boat in terms of economic and social justice.

That was our plan. We decided that Clyde would approach leaders of minority groups in southeastern Michigan, while Ferguson handled the western part of the state. I was a little intimidated about approaching the leaders of those groups, so that was fine with me.

I had secretly admitted at that point that I might be in a little over my head. Plus, I recalled the patronizing treatment I had received from middle-aged leaders in the past, and I knew they would not accept and respect me. So having Clyde and Ferguson carry our water was for the good of the campaign. My main objective was to win.

One of Clyde's first meetings was with the Chaldean Association of America, which is comprised of Iraqis who are non-Muslim. Clyde took me with him and introduced me as the campaign manager. Someone commented that they initially thought I was Clyde's son, and everyone had a little chuckle at my expense.

But I chimed in from time to time with ideas and concerns, something I did whenever I was included in a coalition-building session.

One concern rose above all others every time we held one of those meetings: Does Jesse have a snowball's chance of winning Michigan, much less winning nationally? No one wanted to waste valuable political capital on a loser. Each time that issue came up, we had to out-line a realistic scenario showing how we could win the election. Our position was always that with a coalition of minority voters, plus a sig-nificant contribution from liberal whites, we could win.

That argument became easier to make after the first presidential primaries, when Jesse placed in the top three among nearly ten front-running Democratic hopefuls.

From watching Clyde, I learned that the best approach for dealing with other minority groups was to find out what their hot-button is-sues were, then demonstrate how joining the Jackson campaign could help them address those issues.

I took a one-day break from the campaign during the summer of 1987 to attend my University of Detroit School of Law graduation ceremony. As had been the case at Eastern Michigan University, I walked with the graduating class but still had one course to complete in the fall to finalize things.

In all honesty, getting my law degree wasn't as big an accomplish-ment to me as earning my bachelor's degree had been. Nevertheless, I felt grateful and proud and blessed to be one of a few hundred stu-dents receiving a Juris Doctor degree from the University of Detroit inside a downtown auditorium.

"We've done it again—this is another milestone for us," I told my mother during a moment of quiet reflection.

There was one big difference between getting my bachelor's and my J.D.—my law degree made me feel as though I had a lifetime se-curity. I thought I now possessed a piece of paper that, when com-bined with a law license, could sustain my family and me for the rest of my life.

I felt emancipated, too, because if I ever got fired from my job and no one rehired me, I could always hang out a shingle and make do.

You know the old expression "It takes money to make money." That holds true for the expense of earning a law degree, too. On graduation day I had a debt cloud hanging over me that kept me from owning my law diploma. My debt was a student loan that I had been too poor to pay. It would take me two years to pay what I owed so I could hold my diploma for the first time.

I plunged back into the job of running Jesse's campaign the day after graduation. Those of us pushing Jesse's candidacy had a very hard time recruiting traditional Democratic activists in Detroit, because they were scared to buck the Coleman Young and the UAW machines. So we developed a strategy of sending me out to speak to young people at universities and community colleges throughout Michigan.

I was able to fall back on what I had learned coordinating student rallies at Eastern Michigan. I reached out to the heads of student organizations and sent out several mass mailings. But my primary focus was on minority student organizations.

Jackson made a campaign visit to Detroit while all this was going on, and I scheduled him for an appearance at the Seventh-Day Adventist church I had attended as a child.

My work as the Michigan campaign manager for a major presidential candidate represented a triumphant return of sorts. The church agreed to allow Jesse to come and address the congregation for two to five minutes on the Sabbath, which was Saturday. When he arrived, people were lined up outside the church and onto the sidewalk, and news cameras were everywhere. After the service started, the pastor introduced me to the congregation as "one of our homegrown sons." He reminded people that I had been one of the church's bad boys while growing up, but now I was returning with the first black man to run for president. I received a sustained standing ovation, and it was all I could do to blink back the tears, because I was thinking about Mama the entire time.

I thanked everyone and told them that my mother would have been proud of all of us, and I attributed my success to the training that I had received at that church and at the church school. After my introduction, Jesse came up and hugged me and introduced me as his campaign manager.

With his Secret Service detail and his personal bodyguard looking on, Jesse unleashed a vintage rousing Jacksonian speech. His topic was primarily "Why Do I Run?" and he gave a number of compelling reasons.

Then he was whisked away to another Detroit campaign stop in a big Ford sedan. We made a conscious decision that Jesse was not to ride in a limousine, in keeping with his image as a man of the people.

One aspect of Jesse's personality that complicated my job as Michigan campaign manager is that he's not the most punctual person in the world. As a result, his planned campaign appearances typically started half an hour late. That's because he was always scrambling to do the work of twenty men. Sometimes, a courageous campaign member would attempt to grab Jesse by the elbow and guide him away so he could make his appointments on time. Jesse might look up at you and not respond one way or the other, like you had said nothing at all. He would stare at you for about three seconds with a blank expression on his face, as if he were thinking about something. It used to hurt my feelings until I saw he did it to other campaign workers, too.

While Jesse was in Michigan we had him go on a bus tour that stopped at small to mid-sized cities like Flint, Saginaw, and Lansing that are along the Interstate 75 corridor. There was an awful lot of excitement and electricity in the air statewide regarding Jesse. Especially in Detroit, where I had taken to regularly riding through the city's toughest, poorest neighborhoods with a bullhorn in my hand. Word quickly got out that Jackson had a young street guy going into all the projects and other places that candidates had traditionally ignored.

Instead of relying on a script when using my bullhorn, I talked from the heart about how Jesse had spent his entire adult life standing up for black folks.

I had a sense that I was a part of something historic, which excited me tremendously. The campaign consumed me to the point where I thought about it all the time and was devoting fifteen-hour days to it.

XI

FATHERHOOD

Jesse had already won Democratic presidential primaries in several southern states, and I had a growing sense that he would be able to add Michigan to his win column. Not only was I tremendously proud to be associated with his Michigan presidential drive—here I was managing the campaign. I had to pinch myself from time to time to make sure I wasn't dreaming.

While all this was going on, somehow I still found the time to attend my one law school course. I had taken to camping out in the rear of the classroom with my legal pad and various Jackson campaign documents spread across my desk. On more than one occasion I would be looking at the professor and nodding, but thinking about campaign strategy the whole time.

Meanwhile Linda was waddling around comically. She looked like she was ready to deliver in September 1987, even though her due date was the following month. I really wish I could say I was there for her while she carried our first child, but I was too heavily involved in the Jackson campaign to be of much use. Throughout her pregnancy, Linda continued to work as a director and teacher in a preschool, the

Bates Academy for the Gifted. I learned to appreciate my wife even more during this grueling period in our lives.

People had warned me that it would be very difficult—if not impossible—for me to manage a presidential campaign, attend law school, keep my job at City Hall, and assist my wife through her pregnancy. They were right, because I was totally overwhelmed.

That's part of the reason I had decided to only take one course at law school. At work, Clyde was very understanding in terms of allowing me to downsize my workload for the city council.

So my primary focus was Jesse's campaign, and making sure that my wife had a healthy and safe pregnancy and delivery. Whenever possible, I arrived home by eight or nine in the evening so I could spend some time with Linda in the two-family house we bought that year.

In September, I started going to Lamaze class with her at the hospital where she was supposed to deliver. I was usually able to stay in Lamaze class only about ten minutes before my Jackson campaign pager would go off and I'd go sprinting down a hospital corridor in search of a pay phone. But Linda was always very understanding and accommodating, because she believed strongly in what I was doing and was supportive of it. We had a very strong family support system as well, made up of her parents and her sisters.

In the last two weeks of September, Linda experienced a host of medical complications, including anemia, and had to be hospitalized. So in the days leading to the birth of my first child I was running back and forth between Jackson's Michigan campaign headquarters on Detroit's West Side and the hospital where Linda was.

I spent the night in the hospital a couple of times, because I had become frightened and concerned. The threat of losing my wife and my child scared the holy shit out of me. Things finally deteriorated to the point where the obstetrician overseeing Linda's pregnancy came in one day and explained it was necessary to perform a cesarean and take out the child.

They decided to do the procedure on October 2, 1987. Late in the evening, the doctor and his medical team delivered a beautiful baby girl. I was prowling around the delivery room when they called me to lay eyes on our firstborn child. Looking contentedly at my daughter, I felt ecstatic to be heading a family of my own, which was something that I had wanted since my mother died nine years earlier.

As I held my itty-bitty child, with her full head of wet, curly black hair, I thought that unlike my father, I was going to have a traditional storybook family and get the fatherhood thing right.

We used a book of African names to choose the name Camara, which means "light in the midst of darkness." Camara's middle name, Alice, comes from my mother.

I wanted more than anything to lavish my undivided attention on my wife and daughter, but given how busy and chaotic my life was, there was no way I could. So it eased my mind considerably when Linda and Camara moved out of our house and into Linda's parents' place for a few weeks.

In March 1988, the evening before Michigan voters were to choose their Democratic representative for the presidential race, Jesse flew into town for a series of meetings where I, Annette Rainwater, Clyde Cleveland, and other members of the Michigan campaign discussed strategy in our storefront headquarters on Detroit's West Side.

He wanted to know what his state prospects were and we told him that although Detroit mayor Coleman Young and the UAW were strong, we thought he had a chance to win the city. When it came to the entire state, we weren't so sure, though.

On election eve, reclining in a large chair with his jacket off, his tie loosened, and his shoes off, the preacher in Jesse emerged. Using parables to illustrate various points, this eloquent black man with the *cojones* to run for president of the United States stressed that we had to keep the faith and take full advantage of the resources available to us.

Every so often he would be interrupted by a phone call and he would segue smoothly into the waiting crisis, talking low and half mumbling. By the time one A.M. rolled around, everyone in the room was tired and practically dead on their feet, but the charisma and electricity flowing off Jesse buoyed us to go the extra yard.

Taking in Jesse's bravura performance, it occurred to me that I had never seen anybody work like him in my entire life. He had to work twenty hours, nonstop, and every time he ate it was during a meeting or at a function. It boggled my mind that he had the energy and the will to work late into the night after a full day of campaigning.

We finally wrapped up and I made it home around two in the morning. Too tired to be nervous or anxious about the upcoming day, I fell asleep immediately and was sleeping soundly when the alarm went off three hours later.

I called my childhood friend Rick, who was also working on the campaign, and told him I'd meet him at our West Side headquarters. Annette Rainwater was already there when we arrived, fussing at people and giving orders.

We had vans that were picking up homeless people and recovering drug addicts whom we paid fifty dollars per person to pass out Jackson campaign literature near polling places around Detroit. Coleman Young and the UAW had already snapped up the activists who traditionally work the polls, so we had to make do.

When the polls closed at eight P.M. I went down to the Michigan Election Commission office to await the official count from the polling districts around the state. We fully expected to win Detroit, which was 75 percent black by then, but we didn't expect to win all of Michigan.

Every now and then I made a phone call to the downtown hotel suite where Jesse, Clyde, and Ferguson were holed up as the results began to come in. After reporting my count, I'd ask what the press was reporting about the Michigan race. I could give a detailed account of how specific trees looked, but I couldn't watch television and get a sense of how the Michigan electoral forest appeared.

Back in Jesse's hotel suite, they heard that we stood an excellent chance of winning the entire state! By midnight the final count for Detroit made our victory a sure thing, and all the Jackson campaign workers flocked to our headquarters to celebrate.

Amid all the television cameras and volunteers and poll workers jammed into the small headquarters elbow to elbow, there was a sense of history in the air. Michigan was by far the biggest state, and the only northern state, Jackson had won in either of his presidential campaigns. And I was his campaign manager!

Members of the media rushed to me the moment they recognized who I was.

"Looks as though Reverend Jackson is going to make history and win the state of Michigan. What are you feeling?"

I shot off a stock platitude about hard work paying off, and said that if you built a rainbow coalition among grassroots people and folks who had historically been neglected by society, it gives you a strong shot at winning.

The magnitude of what we had just pulled off was a little too great for me to instantly get my arms around it and then spit out a fully formed sound bite for the press. I was numb, and I looked at all the crying and hugging people around me as if I were a zombie.

Then Jesse's car and the Secret Service glided up to the front door and the media rushed out the door to catch Jesse stepping out of his car. As frenzied as the campaign headquarters was before that, it turned into a madhouse at that instant. People were going crazy, chanting "Keep hope alive," and pushing each other.

I went to sleep that night knowing that I had played a significant role in one of the most noteworthy moments in modern black history. My thoughts went to my mother and the time I told her that I had met Jesse Jackson. I recalled that she told me that if I went to college, I might have a chance to work with Jesse.

After Jesse's historic victory, a number of local newspaper pieces appeared that detailed my role in the campaign. At the University of Detroit School of Law, I received grudging and heartfelt congratulations for having helped guide Jesse to a victory that few thought was possible.

Of course, I never heard a peep out of Andre. I'm sure he was too busy pushing poison in our community to even notice.

In March 1988 a close friend, Cornell Moorman, and I both submitted applications to be admitted to the Michigan bar. We both had grown up in Detroit and had so many similarities in our backgrounds that we naturally gravitated to each other. Like me, Cornell had received an advanced degree from the university of the streets before attending Eastern Michigan University after being paroled from prison. After attending different law schools, we found it amusing that the parallel universes we lived in were again intersecting.

Cornell had applied to be admitted to Michigan's bar before me, and he alerted me that the state bar's character and fitness committee wanted to interview him. That request alarmed us.

Once you've put yourself through the rigors, sacrifices, and bullshit that accompany law school, the last thing you want is an obstruction on the path to getting a law license. A legal degree without admission to the bar generally isn't worth the parchment paper it's printed on.

Some of my fears were allayed, however, when Cornell informed me that the board quizzed him for about fifteen minutes, applauded him for turning his life around, and suggested that he lecture inner-city youth about his inspirational journey. That was all it took for Cornell to be granted his law license, and his childhood record was worse than mine.

Cornell had served a little over two years in prison for a criminal offense that took place when he was in his late twenties. I was very hopeful that because I hadn't served a jail term as long as his, and because my crimes weren't quite as serious and were committed when I was a teenager, getting admitted to the bar should be a breeze for me as well.

In April 1988 I was called before the character and fitness committee for my interview. It was held in the prestigious law offices of the attorney who was chairing the panel at the time. I was ushered into a fancy conference room where the four attorneys who were to judge my character were already seated. The committee consisted of a white female, two white males, and one black male. Acting as if they had a plane to catch, they began raking me over the coals as soon as I was in my seat.

"You're here because there are some concerns regarding your background, and our job is to determine whether you have the character and fitness to be a member of the state of Michigan bar," said the chairman, who was one of the two white males.

As he spoke, his expression was so stern I expected him to break into a recitation of my Miranda rights. The other three looked at me piercingly, their eyes seeming to say, What kind of nigger are you, anyway?

They asked if I cared to make an opening statement about myself and why, despite my troubled past, I should be admitted. Cornell had warned me they would want that kind of statement, so I had outlined one to give to my inquisitors. Basically, my statement was a brief history of my life and was as frank and open as I could make it.

I began to read my statement and hadn't been speaking twenty seconds before the white female lawyer, who appeared to be about forty and was wearing expensive-looking threads, interrupted.

"Mr. Mathis, why did you have such an extensive criminal record as a youth?" she asked brusquely.

"My environment had a lot to do with my troubles as a young man, but once I left that environment, my troubles ended," I replied.

"Yes, but many thousands of people grow up in that environment, yet they don't engage in criminal activity," she replied in a confrontational way.

I remained outwardly calm, but I knew damn well she had no first-hand knowledge of the environment I had described or how one might be affected by it. So how in the hell could she possibly challenge what I was telling her?

She'd never lived it—I doubt that she'd even visited it. I felt utter contempt for that stylishly dressed, privileged woman and was pissed she would be so arrogant and presumptuous as to tell me how my surroundings should have affected me while I was growing up!

However, if there was ever a venue in which I definitely needed to keep my explosive temper reigned, this was it. I could feel the eyes of the three male lawyers on my face as they carefully scrutinized my reaction.

Alarms were going off in my mind, because I was beginning to sense that my path to a law license wasn't going to be anywhere near as smooth as Cornell's. As soon as I concluded my remarks, I began hearing questions in surround sound. The brother spoke up first, in what I now think was an attempt to smooth the way for me. "You have been able to overcome your rough start as a kid and have in your adult years turned yourself around and made good," he said. "Why do you think you were able to do that when so many others, as you stated, haven't?"

I replied that I believed the early foundation of spirituality, morality, and education that my mother instilled in me proved to be my saving grace. It allowed me to survive and overcome my environment.

The black attorney nodded his head as I spoke. It was beginning to be apparent that the brother was in my camp, but the white committee members clearly weren't.

The white woman jumped in again.

"I see here on your record that you were arrested for several crimes," she said in a voice that was stern and totally without compassion. "Tell me what occurred and what were the circumstances surrounding these arrests." Her tone and demeanor made me feel as though I was on the witness stand, fielding questions designed to make me lose my composure.

Visibly irritated and more than a little indignant, I proceeded as best I could to describe the circumstances surrounding each arrest, ranging from purse snatchings to burglaries.

One of the white males served up another test for my patience when he noted that I appeared to blame most of my childhood crimes on my friends and environment. Did I hold myself accountable for any of my actions?

The other white male followed with: "Can you comfortably say that you're one hundred percent rehabilitated at this point?"

"Yes," I said, yielding to the temptation to be sarcastic. "I don't think I'll be breaking into any more houses any time soon."

Next I was quizzed about my traffic tickets and delinquent debts, and whether those things demonstrated a lack of full rehabilitation, as well as dishonesty. The brother sat quietly while this negative bombardment took place.

I was good and damned steamed when the board dispersed and notified me that I would hear of their decisions within thirty days. In fact, the report didn't come for another six agonizing months.

After Jesse Jackson's success in Michigan, his national campaign workers asked if I wanted to go to a couple of Midwestern states on Jesse's behalf. Despite having a new baby, I immediately said yes. The almost narcotic excitement of being associated with the campaign had me hooked.

Unfortunately, instead of working for two consecutive weeks, as I had been told I would, I was essentially flown into a couple of states on successive weekends. I found that experience frustrating because I was essentially standing on the sidelines while the action swirled all around me.

On the heels of that disappointment came an interesting development: I was selected to be one of Michigan's delegates for the Democratic National Convention, which would take place in Atlanta in July 1988. My selection made me the youngest Michigan delegate to attend the 1988 Democratic convention.

Right before the Democratic convention rolled around, Cornell Moorman and I took a little jaunt eighty-eight miles northwest of De-

troit to Lansing, Michigan, the state capital. The purpose of our journey was to take the state bar exam; I had been preparing for several
weeks by studying a bar review book.

However, as soon as that two-day test got under way, it was clear
to me that my preparation wasn't sufficient. Cornell wasn't thrilled by
the way the bar exam had played out, either, and we spent the entire
return trip to Detroit railing against the system. "We've been through
all these years of law school—why the hell do we have to take a bar
exam anyway?"

I didn't have long to reflect on that disappointment because I immediately headed off to Atlanta and the Democratic National Convention. Jesse Jackson had most Democratic delegates allotted to
Michigan, thanks to having won the state's presidential primary. In
addition to myself, Annette Rainwater, Clyde Cleveland, Joel Ferguson, and about twenty other people associated with Jackson's Michigan campaign were also Atlanta-bound.

In a show of unity, we decided to grant Coleman Young's people a
portion of our delegates. Linda, who by the time of the convention
was pregnant again, flew down to Atlanta with me.

The convention marked my first encounter with Ron Brown, who
at the time was Jesse's convention manager. He carried our water,
so to speak, in negotiations with the Democratic party's top power
brokers.

Those of us backing Jackson knew doggone well we didn't have
enough delegates to win the presidential nomination, which went to
Democratic Massachusetts governor Michael Dukakis. So Jackson's
people wanted to make damn sure that the party platform included
issues important to black people, because in the past Democrats had
ignored our issues and taken our votes for granted.

If our issues weren't addressed, we wanted Jesse to be named the
vice-presidential nominee. We let it be known that if we failed to
achieve either of those objectives, we weren't supporting the Democratic ticket.

My first impression of Brown, who went on to become chairman of the Democratic National Committee and then secretary of commerce, was that he was an erudite member of the black bourgeoisie who knew his way around the white Democratic power structure.

Initially, I wasn't sure whether we could trust him. However, I knew that we needed someone like him who had relationships with the Democratic establishment if we were to have any hopes of moving up to another level of activism. Most of our delegates and campaign officials were on the grassroots level or were Democratic party outsiders who didn't know the plays or the players well enough to get us where we needed to be.

The mood within the Jackson camp was very tense, because black businessmen and members of the black middle class who supported Jesse were fearful of being separated from the Democratic mainstream. They had a valid point because if Republican candidate George Bush were elected, we'd have four more years of Reaganomics. Therefore, we had no real choice but to support Dukakis.

During our meetings, which were attended by several hundred people, there was a great deal of acrimonious infighting and people screaming "Sellout!" at the top of their lungs. I was fascinated by this process and by its intensity.

Through Ron Brown's negotiations, we were able to secure some concessions from the Democratic party and the Dukakis people. At first they resisted all our suggestions, so we said, "Okay, you win it by yourself. We're going to walk out!" We were playing a high-stakes poker game.

I enjoyed watching Brown operate. The very top button of his immaculately starched shirts was always fastened, making it look as if he were on the verge of being choked to death. He carried himself in a way that was highly professional and sophisticated. The brother had a tremendous amount of class and self-assurance.

His efforts reaffirmed a suspicion I had that working within the system could be just as effective, if not more effective, than working against it from the outside.

One of the concessions Brown wrangled was permission for Jesse to address the Democratic convention during prime time. The incredible passion and eloquence Jesse displayed drove even non-Jackson delegates to tears. He talked about how those who lived in barrios and ghettoes and those who called Appalachia home all had the same goals, objectives, and obstacles in life. And that we needed to unite under one big tent, one big rainbow coalition.

As everyone knows, the Democrats went on to lose to George Bush in the fall of 1988. However, shortly afterward Ron Brown was named chairman of the Democratic National Committee and the number of blacks on the committee increased significantly.

Thinking back on it, Jesse Jackson should have been the Democrats' vice-presidential nominee. I'm still convinced to this day that he would have given Dukakis a better chance to beat Bush.

After I returned to Detroit, it felt odd to only have my family and my City Hall job to concentrate on. With law school and the Jackson campaign now in my past, a degree of routine returned to my life that hadn't been there for quite some time.

While I could certainly do without law school, I missed the cut and thrust of working with Jesse's campaign. Being intimately involved with politics on a national scale had been heady stuff, and I would have welcomed an opportunity to get plugged back into that scene.

Around the same time the end-of-year holiday season arrived, so did a slim envelope from the state bar of Michigan. I opened the envelope and learned that I had failed the bar exam.

Furthermore, I still hadn't heard back from the Michigan bar character and fitness committee that I had appeared before five months ago—the same panel that had promised to get back to me in thirty days!

Once you let self-doubt and self-pity creep into your psyche, they tear away at you like acid. My hopes of becoming a lawyer were quickly dwindling, putting me into something of a free fall.

When anyone looked at me, though, outwardly they saw the bright young up-and-comer who had helped Jesse Jackson to a historic victory in Michigan and who had completed law school after rescuing himself from a life of crime. I'm a very private person, so no one knew the complete anguish and despair I felt inside.

I even kept it from Linda to a large degree, because I didn't want her to think the man in her life—the father of her children, the family provider—was weak. I had to let her in, though, after that Michigan bar panel finally came back with its report.

In essence, the three-page report tore me a new ass. It claimed that I had a general disregard for the law and for authority and was unable to distinguish right from wrong. The committee saw me as someone who was always trying to excuse and rationalize my behavior, instead of accepting responsibility or accountability.

Internally I played a little mind game with myself and took on the attitude that my rejection wasn't that big a deal, because I had already defied the odds to get to where I was in life.

But I couldn't fool my body. It knew that I was angry as hell over having done what the system wanted me to do and still having gotten the shaft. Judge Kaufman had asked me to get a GED, and I had gone a lot further than that. I believed that I had a lot to offer society as a productive citizen. There was no doubt in my mind that I had redeemed myself and had repaid my debt to society, having provided nearly ten years of public service.

I was headed for depression, plus I was plagued by indigestion and chronic heartburn. I hid my symptoms from Linda. When I didn't eat, it was because I didn't want to gain weight or because I was seeking a "healthier lifestyle." When I had to deal with gas, it was a simple matter to go into a different part of the house. What man wants to be viewed as some weak-stomach punk by his wife? I certainly didn't. Linda undoubtedly heard my stomach rumbling like a volcano all the time, and had to notice my short temper and surly, withdrawn personality. Eventually things got to the point where I had to see a doctor, who diagnosed me as having stress-induced gastritis and acid reflux.

I could see Andre's sardonic sneer and hear his taunting words inside my head. "See, the system ain't cut out for us, Scoey. Tole ya that shit, but you wouldn't listen!"

Deciding to give the establishment another chance, I applied for a civil servant job down at City Hall. I did it quietly, too, because I didn't want to let Clyde and Rainwater know how badly my confidence had been rattled. I went for a job as a financial analyst that paid $15 an hour, as opposed to the $7.50 an hour I was making.

The interview process went well and I made it past the first round of cuts, then survived the second round of dismissals to be granted a third and final interview. It was with a woman named Bella Marshall, who was the director of the finance department and one of Mayor Coleman Young's closest aides.

She was on the verge of hiring me when she noticed that I hadn't completed the section of the employment application asking if I had ever been convicted of a crime. She asked me if that happened to be an oversight and was also curious if I had passed the bar.

I felt it would be best if I gave Mrs. Marshall full and complete disclosure, thinking that being a sister, she would understand. But she didn't, and she immediately told me that she couldn't hire me. She pointed out all the troubles that Coleman Young was already having with his department heads and other political appointees being investigated by his enemies.

Shit, will the bad news ever stop? I can't even be a damn bureaucrat, I thought to myself. My morale had hit rock bottom.

I had a conversation with my mother's sister, Aunt Ethel, who had always been a spiritual, God-fearing woman and who had recently moved from Cleveland to Detroit following the death of her husband. As Aunt Ethel saw it, I had been moving away from my faith, so she suggested that I attend her church in Detroit, Ebenezer A.M.E.

I figured, why not? My stomach hurt all the time and I was a law school graduate making a ridiculous $7.50 an hour.

So my family and I joined Ebenezer A.M.E., and I began praying regularly to strengthen my faith in God and in myself. I just didn't know what else to do.

There was nothing great about the services at Ebenzer and they didn't have the power I needed, but the prayer seemed to help. This was all about me finding sanctuary in religion. I was going to confront my enemies with prayer, because I felt that I could put it on God again. I was going to give God one more chance.

XII

WHAT'S IN A NAME?

I was determined not to let Linda's second pregnancy get away from me the way the first one had. This time I took some Christmas vacation just to be with my family. Linda, Camara, and I spent a lot of time during the holidays at Linda's parents' home in suburban Detroit.

Linda and I knew that our next child was going to be a boy, so we had a little naming issue to deal with: What should we name our son?

My buddies and I had always contended that when you make a boy a "junior," his success is dependent on his father's name and success. So we had always said that if we had sons, we were going to force them to make it on their own.

On the one hand I wanted to name my son after me, but on the other hand that would go against what I had previously stated about naming a boy Junior. I decided to look into the matter further, and had a conversation with a young brother who had been named after his father, the highest-ranking African American in the United Auto Workers union.

Horace Sheffield said that being a junior had proved to be a double-edged sword in his life. On the one hand, being the progeny of a powerful father had made it possible for Horace to meet Dr. Martin Luther King several times as a child and had allowed him to become the youngest school board member in Detroit history at the age of twenty-one.

The flip side was that Horace had always been criticized by some of his peers and competitors who alleged that his success was only a result of his father's name. When that happened, Horace said he would tell his detractors that it wasn't his fault their father wasn't shit!

Upon hearing that, I decided I was going to name my son after me. And if anybody ever criticized him, I would tell him what Horace Sheffield told me.

Gregory Mathis Jr. was born in Detroit on January 31, 1989.

The following month I got a call from Larry Simmons, the political director for Detroit mayor Coleman Young. The mayor had been quite impressed with my work on Jesse Jackson's presidential campaign, Larry said, and wanted to see if I would be interested in working on his upcoming mayoral campaign.

My immediate question was "How much does it pay?" Larry responded that the salary would be somewhere between twenty and thirty dollars an hour. Hmmm. I was making $7.50 an hour working in the office of City Councilman Clyde Cleveland, and the financial analyst job that I had such high hopes for paid only fifteen an hour.

"Hey, Larry, I'll be glad to meet with the mayor," I said, trying to keep from laughing.

I immediately ran the job offer past Annette Rainwater, who had invested so much time and energy in me and my career. When I told her how much it paid, she said, "Sheeiittt, hell yeah! Take that position, boy!"

"But what would Jesse think?" I asked, genuinely concerned.

"Fuck them motherfuckers—they ain't gonna do shit for ya," Annette said immediately. "Don't worry about anybody thinking that you're being disloyal or switching sides. Just remember that in politics, there are no permanent enemies and no permanent friends."

So I made an appointment to meet with the mayor to discuss the position of citywide coordinator, which was the number-three position in his campaign.

Coleman Young's office was on the eleventh floor of City Hall, two floors below the floor I had worked on for so many years. An intimidating figure, Young was easily the most powerful big-city mayor in America at that time. He was a take-no-prisoners politician who crushed anyone opposed to his aims or points of view.

I was excited about meeting him, as well as nervous and intimidated. I was also haunted by the fact that I had a criminal record and the knowledge that one of his top aides knew. At the same time, I felt if anyone could overlook my past and accept me anyway it would be Coleman Young. Legend had it that he served as a numbers man in his earlier years. He was supposed to have some big numbers men and gangsters around Detroit that he associated with from time to time. Whether or not the legend was true, it certainly added to the mayor's reputation.

On the day I was to meet with Young I made it a point to arrive ten minutes early, so I could hang out in the reception area of the mayor's office and not take the chance of being late. A number of aides scurrying back and forth recognized me and were curious what had brought me to the seat of power on the eleventh floor.

When Young's secretary came over to me and said, "The mayor will see you now," a number of eyes nearly bugged out.

Not surprisingly, Young had a large office that was dominated by a huge desk, a big black leather chair, and plenty of plaques on the walls. Out the window was a terrific view of the Detroit River and Windsor, Canada, which was on the other side of the river.

By this time Young was in his late sixties but still meticulously dressed, with gray hair that was well groomed. He was sporting a tie pin, and was trim and tall with a very light complexion.

When I was introduced to him, Young chuckled as he clasped my hand. "So, *you* the little muthafucker that kicked our ass!"

His comment put me at ease immediately. I felt like he was one of the brothers from the 'hood, and I knew we were going to get along. Young had the air of a mafia don, if you will. That's the vibe I felt from him, like *The Godfather*. I could tell that he was a man at ease with his power and with himself.

He also had a healthy sense of humor, judging from the wooden MR. MOTHERFUCKER! nameplate perched on his desk.

"The number-one thing I require out of anyone working for or with me is loyalty," Young told me after we'd been seated. "Can you remain loyal to me after working for those other motherfuckers?" Meaning Jesse Jackson and Councilman Clyde Cleveland, whom Young hated.

"Mr. Mayor, I've been committed to working for the benefit of the community, not so much for the politicians involved," I said. "Whomever I work for at the time, that's where my loyalties are."

I didn't like the expression that comment brought to Young's face, so at that point I dropped Annette Rainwater's name, too. I had a sense that he liked Rainwater, because when she and I had encountered Young a year earlier, Annette and the mayor had laughed and joked and exchanged pleasantries. Unlike Young's last encounter with Clyde, which led to them getting involved in a profane shouting match on the first floor of City Hall.

Young was still looking at me funny, trying to figure me out. "How did you get into politics? Your parents?"

I related that my mother was deceased and that I really didn't know much about my dad, before launching into the story of how I'd gotten involved in politics. Young listened attentively, his forehead furrowed.

"What high school did you go to?"

"I went to a couple of high schools, but I really didn't finish. I had to get a GED."

Naturally Young wanted to know why, and his tone of voice changed somewhat. I could have kicked myself in the butt for not just mentioning a high school and letting it go at that. I wasn't sure if he knew about my background already and was fishing to see if I would

lie, so I went ahead and laid everything on the table. Jail, getting suspended from schools, everything.

I also mentioned that I had already met the mayor twelve years
earlier, when he attended a street gang summit at the Cobo Hall convention center in a bid to squelch gang-related violence. A youth-
training program that had been one of Young's initiatives helped turn
my life around, too, I told him, because that program made it possible for me to obtain a GED.

Young's mouth flew open at that one. I had a feeling one of two
things would happen from that point forward—he would toss me out
of his office or I would wind up getting the job.

He suddenly broke into a big smile and said, "Your little ass became a lawyer and you did all this political shit after going through
that program I created!"

The mayor of Detroit stood up from his chair and walked around
his desk to where I sat. "Man, get your ass over here and give me a
hug," he cried out with a mixture of joy and pride in his voice.

"I knew you young motherfuckers could do something other than
fuck with people," Young said after giving me a hard embrace. "Shit,
brothers like you from the street can outperform these white boys in
mainstream America any day, because the streets teach you to be resourceful.

"But those silver-spoon motherfuckers, all they do is lay back and
chase pussy and do as little as possible and they get everything. Did
you know I was from the streets, too?"

I was still standing in front of Young, grinning in disbelief at the incredible turn our meeting had taken.

"Yeah, Mr. Mayor," I replied. "They say you used to run the Black
Bottom section of town when you was a young guy."

"Who you been talking to?" Young said, looking surprised I would
know that part of his background. I named some old-timers around
town that I had been talking to.

"I like you, I like you," Young said, laughing and beaming. "You
my kind of motherfucker! I want you to work with Larry Simmons

and Charlie Williams, my campaign manager. My only concern was your loyalty and I know if you're from the streets, you know about loyalty. You work with these gentlemen on the campaign, and we'll go from there."

Young's secretary peeked through the door to his office at that moment. "Mr. Mayor, your other appointment is here."

I shook Coleman Young's hand before I left and he got up from his desk again and put his arm around my shoulder as I was walking out.

During my meeting with the mayor, I had begun to feel that somehow God or my mother was directing my life. I felt everything I had done or experienced had been laid out by fate, and that I was headed toward some kind of leadership role in the black community.

I mean, look at what was going on—it couldn't have been a coincidence! I had become the top aide in Michigan for arguably the most powerful black man in the world, a man who had encouraged me to go to college a decade before I helped guide him to the biggest political victory of his life.

Now, I had just become a top aide for arguably the most powerful black elected official in America, twelve years after meeting and going through a program of his that helped me make the transition from street gang member to productive citizen.

So I left Young's office thinking, Damn, I'm destined to be somebody!

I caught the elevator back up to the thirteenth floor, where Rainwater and I agreed that I needed to tell Clyde Cleveland right away that I'd be leaving his office. I was concerned about how to break the news to Clyde, so I tried to put it off, but as it turned out, things resolved themselves two days later.

Clyde, who has a wicked temper like me, went off on me over a mass mailing we were about to send to some community groups. It was really a minor deal; we just happened to disagree over the language in the letter we were sending out.

However, out of nowhere one of Detroit's most powerful city councilmen began yelling at me and belittling me.

"Just do what I say, just do what I say," he snapped inside his office, as I looked at him, dumbfounded. "I'm the damn councilman—you ain't nobody. If it wasn't for me, you'd be out there with the rest of these little starving law clerks. Just do what the hell I say!"

Well, Clyde's tirade and his words really hurt me. I left his office and returned to my desk and just sat there for about five minutes. On the spot I determined that day would be my last as an employee of Clyde Cleveland.

No one knew it at the time, but Clyde was in the beginning stages of diabetes. Many people who are experiencing the initial phases of the disease are subject to extreme mood swings. Naturally, diabetes was the furthest thing from my mind. All I knew was that Clyde had gone off on me like a madman in front of my coworkers. So I started emptying my desk and putting my stuff in boxes. Some of my colleagues watched in silence as I did this, not eager to jeopardize their own jobs.

By the time I had all my things packed away, I was the one whose temper was boiling. So I decided to give Clyde a piece of my mind back to him.

He had left his office by then and had gone down to the council chambers, where the nine council members create city ordinances while their aides and audience members look on. With the city council in session, I came stalking into chambers.

"Clyde!" I bellowed across the room. Every single person looked up in amazement.

"You can take this job and shove it up your motherfucking ass," I shouted. "Who in the fuck do you think you were talking to me like that? I'm not one of those women in the office you've been going off on every day—I'll shoot you in the top of your motherfucking head!"

By this time the city council's armed security detail, who knew me, had entered the chambers and grabbed me. "Come on, Greg, don't do this, man," one of them said.

But I wasn't hearing what they had to say—all I could see was Clyde Cleveland and the goofy look of astonishment he was wearing.

"Get up, get up now, bitch!" I continued, refusing to let up. "You wanna do something? I'll whip your ass *right now!*"

"Just go, man," Clyde said, finally getting over his shock. "Just get your fucking stuff and GO!"

City Councilman Clyde and I wouldn't speak to each other for another three or four years. He cannily got the last word in that dispute, and he did so by hitting me hard where I lived. He wrote me a letter claiming that he planned to notify the Detroit Police Department and the Federal Bureau of Investigation of my threat to harm him with a firearm.

Given that the city council chambers were filled with witnesses, Clyde would have had no trouble following through with that threat. I started praying, begging God not to allow my temper and big mouth to ruin my chances of getting on Mayor Young's staff. Threatening Clyde in a city council chamber filled with potential witnesses hadn't been the brainiest move on my part.

Apparently Clyde was still pissed, and possibly a little afraid, because two days later I got another letter warning that he would report my threat to the state bar if anything happened to him. I can assure you that Clyde's second letter grabbed my attention to an even greater degree than the first one.

I quickly got on the phone and called Rainwater. I told her to tell Clyde that I was sorry about losing my temper and that he didn't have to worry about me giving him any trouble. Apparently that did the trick, because his irate correspondence to me stopped.

XIII

MR. MF!

It was a relief to begin working with Mayor Coleman Young, because the job paid considerably more than my old position in Clyde Cleveland's office. I came on board with the title of citywide campaign coordinator, and my mission was to organize various Detroit constituency groups behind the mayor's reelection bid.

This meant I was to preach the Young gospel to churches, community groups, block clubs, lawyers, and young professionals. That last group was critically important, because Young's primary challenger was a young black millionaire named Tom Barrow, who happened to be the nephew of boxing great Joe Louis. Barrow had money and the backing of the media and the white establishment, but he didn't have grassroots support. Having seen my performance in the Jackson presidential campaign, Young's people felt I could deliver that last element.

I was walking into the middle of what was being billed as Young's most difficult campaign, following sixteen years in office. Just being in office that many years causes voters to start to tire of you.

In what was to become my hallmark achievement in Young's reelection campaign, over a six-month period I organized ten social gatherings for young professionals. The average attendance was five hundred people and a couple of those affairs had as many as two thousand people.

After paying ten dollars to get in, partygoers would get live music, hors d'oeuvres and a campaign message delivered by me during intermission. They also got to enjoy themselves at the most sought-after social gatherings in Detroit during 1989.

During the Jackson campaign, my associations had been pretty much limited to the grassroots crowd. But when I was working for Young, my activities put me in touch with the black establishment. I was now rubbing shoulders with the people I'd felt rejected by most of my life. Some of them were actually kissing my behind in a bid to get in good with Detroit's political power structure.

As I immersed myself in the Young campaign, for the first time in my life I was on solid footing financially and professionally. Linda had started operating a second preschool by 1989, and I was widely referred to as a rising political star.

One evening my friend from childhood Rick and I were in a club passing out invitations to one of my "Coleman Young for Mayor" soirees. Who should be in the club but Andre, who was sitting at a corner table with his boys and their women.

As usual, jewelry was dangling everywhere and a couple of bottles of Dom Perignon on ice were sitting on the table.

"Whassup, Scoey? Whatchoo doing now, man?" Andre said, laughing and immediately beginning to marginalize me. "Come here, come here, man."

I walked over to Andre's table, wondering if he had managed to think up an original put-down by now.

"These muthafuckas got you out here passing out flyers!" Andre said derisively. "I know you didn't go to law school for this. Scoey, you been going to school about ten years now, haven't you? Damn, this politics game is slow."

"Fuck you, Andre." I laughed.

I got the last chuckle when Young was able to defeat Barrow by a margin of 52 percent to 48 percent. It was the mayor's smallest margin of victory since his original election, and I think I played an instrumental role in helping him win.

Once Young's reelection campaign ended in November, my job ended with it. I kept calling City Hall to see if the mayor had compiled a list of appointees, but each time I was told the list wasn't finished. This went on until the beginning of February, when I was finally notified what my position within Young's administration would be.

I was offered the job of city hall manager for Detroit's East Side City Hall. Detroit maintains regional city halls so that residents can inquire about services and register complaints without having to travel all the way downtown.

Many people thought that job offer was not what I deserved, because the smart money had me working as an executive assistant in the mayor's office. When that didn't materialize, word flew around town that I'd gotten a bullshit assignment.

I felt slighted at first, but when I know I can't fight a situation I always flip the script and find a way that it will benefit me. So I decided to use my city hall manager position as a base to get into elective office after four years.

The job paid $45,000 a year, I had a city car at my disposal, and I oversaw a staff of four.

My position would hardly be a cakewalk, either, because much of the East Side was inside an area known as the most impoverished congressional district in the country. The East Side had a reputation as the toughest, poorest, and oldest part of Detroit. In addition to poverty, there's also drug abuse, crime, a lack of education, and the city's highest levels of infant mortality and teen pregnancy.

The East Side Neighborhood City Hall was in a dilapidated, drug- and crime-infested neighborhood at the corner of Mack and Chalmers Avenues. I was very familiar with the corner, because I had hung out there the summer I stayed on the East Side with my father. Next door to the East Side Neighborhood City Hall was a former drugstore whose brick walls were caving in. On the other side was a business where folks could cash welfare checks or paychecks.

I immediately knew my new job would be a huge challenge, because one of the duties was to uplift the neighborhood and provide city services, such as ensuring garbage collection. It appeared that the building I worked in was in greater need of service than the rest of the neighborhood.

I determined to turn what some people viewed as a setback into an advantage by uplifting this grassroots community and its citizens. If I did that, I felt I would always have a loyal group of citizens and voters to support my future ambitions. And I reminded myself that one of my original reasons for getting into politics was to empower impoverished black people.

The other part of my job called for me to act as the mayor's liaison to the East Side, interacting primarily with neighborhood organizations, churches, and businesses. For four straight years, I was at a meeting every night. Not surprisingly, it put a strain on my home life.

I got in every night at nine o'clock, right before the kids went to bed. At seven-thirty the next morning, I'd be out the door, headed back to East Side Neighborhood City Hall, which was a half-hour commute, since Linda and I had stepped out on faith and sold our two-family flat. We bought a two-story colonial home in an upscale part of Detroit called Rosedale Park. We bought it as-is for $60,000 and put $20,000 worth of repairs into it, including two new ceilings.

Let me tell you why I was spending so little time with my family during those years. I had it in my head that while my children were toddlers, I could sacrifice some of my quality time with them. I thought that they might not remember it anyway by the time they had gotten to be adolescents and teenagers.

I also tried to make up for my absences during the week by totally shutting down work on the weekends, from Saturday morning to Monday morning. It was an established fact among my coworkers and my friends not to invite me to anything, not even parties.

I admit it was a selfish strategy, because it called for Linda to be Hercules Monday through Friday, but I was sure that one day it would pay off and Linda would be able to enjoy the fruit of my labors.

My wife and I sometimes felt overwhelmed during the week, and the stress often got to a point where it limited our communication with each other. One point of friction for us was the appearance of our house during that time in our lives. It was hard for Linda to maintain a spotless home and have dinner prepared, because she was operating two preschools twelve hours a day and dealing with our children, and I was of no help to her. Still, I was frustrated with the disorganization in our house, and I'd lash out occasionally, because of my stress and frustration. Then she'd remind me of her responsibilities.

Another flash point revolved around the demands of my career. Sometimes when I got home late, she would angrily ask if I had been out tasting my career, or if I had been tasting something else.

Linda is my soulmate, but we had some verbal throwdowns that were damned ugly during my time at East Side Neighborhood City Hall. So from the standpoint of my home life, we were both relieved when my time at East Side Neighborhood City Hall wound to a close after Young made his retirement public.

During my enforced layoff before getting the East Side appointment, I had used my downtime to bone up for the Michigan bar exam again. This time, I was determined to pass that damned thing.

I came home one day in May 1990 and found the mailman had dropped off another envelope from the Michigan Bar Association. I ripped it open immediately, and the letter read: "We are pleased to inform you . . ." That first sentence was all I needed to see. I started jumping up and down screaming inside my empty house, throwing my fist in the air. Then I fell down to my knees and thanked God once again for my mother. To celebrate, I went out to dinner that night with Linda, who was several months pregnant with our third child.

Two months later, on July 6, 1990, Amir Mathis came into the world. I was concerned about his health, because once again Linda had suffered anemia and they had had to remove him. But once again God smiled on the Mathis family, and neither mother nor child suffered any major complications.

I had four children now, and I needed the kind of income that a law degree could potentially generate. Unfortunately, the Michigan Bar Association's character and fitness committee continued to hold my law license hostage. I had to hire an attorney and go all the way to the Michigan State Supreme Court before finally getting permission to practice law in Michigan. I finally won the struggle to get my law license a year and a half after passing the bar exam.

On the heels of my success with Jesse Jackson's presidential campaign in Michigan and Mayor Coleman Young's victorious reelection campaign, I had an opportunity in 1991 to see if I could use what I had learned to run an election campaign on my own. The candidate was an African American attorney I knew, Leonia Lloyd, who was running for a position as judge with the 36th District Court in downtown Detroit.

Hers was a long-shot campaign, and when I succeeded in getting her elected to the bench, a couple of things became apparent to me. First, it seemed that I actually did have a little Midas touch going on when it came to shepherding political candidates through the electoral process. Second, if I ever decided to run for elective office, I would have a wealth of firsthand know-how for running my own campaign.

I had met Leonia and her twin sister, Leona, through doing part-time work with their Detroit law firm. They referred some of their cases to me and taught me how to handle them in exchange for me taking charge of Leonia's judicial campaign.

Once Leonia was elected I assumed much of her caseload, particularly juvenile and minor cases being heard at the 36th District Court, where she had become a judge. I got referrals from that court and was making about $25,000 a year on the side while still working for the mayor.

One day as I was walking over to the 36th District Court for a hearing, who should I run into coming out of the courthouse but Andre. He was by himself, too, instead of being accompanied by a lawyer or his usual entourage of mental midgets.

Andre was wearing a sweatsuit, and I assumed that he had been to court for a hearing of his own. I was a little apprehensive because we hadn't seen or spoken to each other in a year, and our last encounter hadn't been particularly pleasant.

My longtime antagonist immediately broke into a big smile and yelled out, "Scoey! What's up, man?" We exchanged a high-five as if several years of hard feelings and tension between us had never existed.

"What's up, Andre?"

"Whatchoo doin' down here?" Andre responded, answering my question with a question, something that usually annoys me. This time I was pleased, downright proud, to answer.

"I got a case I'm handling," I said, smirking ever so slightly and watching Andre's face.

"You practicing now?" Andre said with surprise. "Them white folks done gave you your license!"

"Yep, they finally gave it to me."

Andre started grinning, which I didn't like. "Aw man, you should have let me know, because I can send you some cases. You can be my shyster."

"Yeah man, why don't you send me some cases? Watchoo doing down here, anyway? Checking on one of your boys who got a case?"

"Naw man, one of my girls works down here."

Andre and I stood in a courthouse corridor having what was almost a normal conversation. I left feeling a little better about our relationship. But it irked me that he still had the need to view me as an underling, based on his remarks. He thought I could work for him now.

I knew I was doing exactly what I needed to be doing, which was working primarily with juvenile cases. That turned out to be a surprisingly frustrating endeavor, because I came to recognize that the judges had little or no compassion for the young black kids who came before them with nonviolent first time offenses. I immediately saw that most of the judges in the 36th District Court were doing nothing more than warehousing black youths in prison.

Every time I went into that courtroom, I saw myself. I began to develop a there-but-for-the-grace-of-God-go-I feeling, and it bothered me. I had seen through my youth agency, YAAT, that if young adults were given the opportunities and the resources to better themselves, for the most part they turned away from a life of crime and self-destruction.

By 1992 YAAT was attracting grant funding from governmental agencies and from corporations, and it had a full-time executive director and two part-time employees.

The following year, Mayor Coleman Young stunned his supporters and staff by announcing he would not be running for a sixth term—meaning that when he departed office, my primary means of making a living would depart with him.

This was devastating news to many within Young's administration, who apparently thought Young would remain mayor forever, and felt betrayed. But since I was already engaged in the practice of law, I felt confident of being able to keep putting food on my family's table.

Far from worrying about my future, I spent most of 1993 managing the city council campaign of a friend of mine, Brenda Scott. Brenda was a couple of years older than me, and she and I started working in City Hall as administrative assistants around the same time. The main challenge her candidacy posed was having to organize volunteers and put in place a winning political strategy with little or no money. What remained of Coleman Young's political machine was pushing a Young loyalist for the same city council vacancy that Brenda had her eye on. Our opponent had been a department head under Young, her campaign was well organized and financed, and she was favored to win.

I was a little concerned that backing Brenda might be viewed as disloyal to the mayor. On the other hand, Young's machine had left me and many other political appointees in the lurch, and in six months there would be no more machine to be loyal to.

So I was simply getting a jump-start on a future without Coleman Young.

Knowing that we would not have much money and no paid staff, I immediately realized I would have to run a grassroots campaign for Brenda. So my strategy was similar to my Jackson campaign strategy: Go to grassroots organizations.

I had an awful lot riding on Brenda's election. I wanted to enhance my growing reputation as a political power broker in Detroit, and I still had my eye on a future in politics. But I also knew that if Brenda won, I could get a consulting contract with her that would replace that Coleman Young salary I was about to lose.

Brenda won in an upset, beating an opponent who spent $250,000. We had spent $40,000, $8,000 of which I had loaned to Brenda in the last thirty days of the campaign to buy television ads.

As always, Linda was very supportive. I guess she figured that I must know what I was doing by now. She had seen how my politics-related sacrifices usually paid off.

XIV

HERE COMES THE JUDGE

After managing my final successful election on behalf of someone else, I felt I had the foundation, knowledge, and political base to run for office myself. The prize I had in mind was a seat on the 36th District Court.

So in January 1994, I sat down with Linda and Rick for the purpose of using them as sounding boards. The three of us sat around the dining room table of my home, sipping wine and dreaming big dreams. Thinking of my oldest brother, Ron, I took a page out of his book and cautioned everyone that we needed to examine my objective as hard-eyed realists, not through rose-colored glasses.

Rick, who had helped me get Brenda Scott into a city council seat, noted that the biggest obstacle we faced in her election had been money. How in the devil would we raise the cash necessary for a successful judicial campaign? Rick wanted to know.

I told him that I would do for myself exactly what I had done in Coleman Young's last campaign—namely throw a series of political parties that would help me raise funds and support.

Aside from financial concerns, the three of us came to the conclusion that my becoming a judge wasn't outside the realm of possibility. So I began sending letters to friends, family members, and political associates, telling them that I was running for 36th District Court judge.

As a result of that mailing, about 150 people attended a kick-off meeting I had in a downtown luxury apartment right next to City Hall. The media pretty much ignored my candidacy, in part because I hadn't held a press conference yet. That's because Jesse had promised to come to town and hold a press conference with me so I could get maximum mileage out of it. The only power broker at my meeting was Councilwoman Brenda Scott.

Interestingly, none of the Coleman Young appointees I had worked with for four straight years had bothered to come to my kick-off meeting. I attributed that to lack of faith.

American politics is a cash-intensive endeavor, and the expenses start to mount from day one. In addition to paying for light refreshments, I had campaign banners made that were emblazoned with the slogan, STOP CRIME, SAVE OUR YOUTH. That's because the lion's share of crime was being committed by black youth between the ages of fourteen and twenty-five. I also had some lawn signs made up right away; they featured a red octagon like a stop sign against a black background.

From January through November, I was planning to adhere to a regimen that began at seven A.M. and ended at eleven P.M., with intermittent swimming breaks at a downtown fitness club when time permitted. That's because swimming relaxes me, and exercise increases my stamina.

Whenever I could squeeze it in, I would run home and have a brief dinner with my family. One of the things that convinced me that I could pull this schedule off for eleven months was Jackson's presidential campaign. I saw a man twenty years my senior do this for a year and a half. If he could do it for a year and a half going from city to city, I figured I could do it in the same city for eleven months.

By March, I'm still waiting on Jesse to do this press conference with me. He's gotta clear his calendar to come, and it's too early because nobody is paying judicial elections any attention yet anyway. But I'm becoming anxious, because a whisper campaign is going on. And what that campaign is saying is "Greg Mathis has a criminal background in addition to not having practiced law extensively."

No one would have argued that I was your typical candidate for judge. I was clearly unconventional, and I knew that unconventional candidates needed to adopt unconventional tactics. Having watched how Jesse Jackson operated and having seen how his unconventional strategies usually paid off, I figured it was my turn to try.

I began by plastering vacant buildings on main avenues and boulevards with my stop sign banner and placards. There's nothing particularly unusual about that, but no other candidate for judge was doing it as early as March, when I started. I figured that getting the jump on everyone else would go a step further toward establishing name recognition for me.

I also used March to launch a knock-and-drop lawn sign solicitation campaign. Even though the people whose lawns you used didn't know you, if you had ten lawn signs within a one-block radius it created a billboard effect, one that made voters assume that you were a well-liked, popular candidate.

The following month I began campaigning in earnest, again long before my competitors. I primarily did this with friends and relatives, because I couldn't afford to pay campaign workers. About twenty of us went out at a time, knocking on doors and handing out campaign literature. Linda and the kids even went out with me on weekends; it creates a powerful image when potential voters see a candidate and his young family sacrificing their weekend for something they believe strongly in. Anyway, everyone knows that cute little kids are the best friends of someone running for office.

April also marked the month that I started going to community meetings to discuss my candidacy. When there were no meetings to attend, I went to grocery markets in every neighborhood in Detroit. My strategy was to start out in the highest-voting districts, then move to the lowest, then, when election time rolled around, to go back to the highest again to reinforce my message.

When the grocery markets shut down, I moved on to bars and nightclubs. On Wednesdays, Fridays, and Sundays, I hit the late-evening church services. The election was so far out that people tended to listen politely for only a few seconds; then they'd grab some campaign literature and walk off.

More often than not, I saw my materials flow into the first waste receptacle the person passed. But knowing that you can't reach everyone, I wasn't discouraged. My goal was to shake 150,000 hands all over Detroit between January and November.

By July, I began to throw fund-raising parties like those I had arranged for Coleman Young's mayoral campaign. Two groups that were particularly helpful in this regard were Men of Wall Street, led by my old friend Sherman Eaton, and The Big Fellas Association, led by Larry Murph. Between the two of them, these brothers were responsible for sending fifteen hundred people to my campaign events.

By now my opponents were starting to take my oddball candidacy seriously, and I began to see them campaigning at churches and before community groups. From time to time, they would mention that some nonincumbents just didn't have the experience necessary to be a good judge, and, without mentioning me by name, they would allude to candidates with backgrounds unbecoming of a judge. My opponents played into my hands whenever they did this, because they unwittingly helped raise my profile, and they invariably pushed my motivation and determination up a notch.

In August, Andre was indicted on charges that he had been participating in a major Detroit drug ring. The cops had been watching him for more than a year and had amassed tape recordings and pictures of his activities.

Even though we had been rivals, I still felt that I had lost another close friend to the war in the streets, another victim of the poverty and hopelessness that impede the progress of so many black men who attempt to overcome the racism and obstacles that are ever-present in this society.

Andre was convicted the same month that I was elected. He ultimately received a sentence of fifteen to thirty years. He's now somewhere in the federal prison system.

I didn't hook up with my esteemed mentor and friend, Jesse Jackson, until October, a month before my big election. He was in Detroit on business, and I quickly threw together a script for him to read at a local radio station.

The brilliance of the man is such that he never laid eyes on that script until we were in the recording studio. Then he read what I had written word-for-word with passion and in only one take.

I ended up buying about ten thousand dollars in radio time, and I also used Jesse's voiceover to make a cheap television campaign ad. It showed me walking in front of City Hall and ran only the night before the election, because that's all I could afford.

I paid five thousand dollars for twelve television ads that ran on two stations.

The night before voters were to decide if I had what it took to be a judge, or if I had been playing with myself for eleven months, my adrenaline just wouldn't let me rest. I suffer from insomnia from time to time, and I didn't drift off until two A.M.

My alarm went off two and a half short hours later. Linda wished me luck, then I went into my children's bedrooms and kissed them while they were asleep.

Before walking out the door, I fell to my knees in prayer.

"God, you know my heart, you know my desires, you know what I'm trying to do. I ask that you bless me in my endeavors today and I ask that you strengthen me, so that I can be a blessing to others."

That night, after the final votes had been tallied, I had beaten the twenty-year incumbent by ten thousand votes. We later discovered that he spent more than $150,000, while I spent less than $40,000.

Seventeen years after getting out of the Wayne County Jail, which sits across from the 36th District Court where I would be presiding, I had become the youngest elected judge in Michigan history. My annual salary was to be $98,000.

After traversing an incredibly arduous path to become a judge, it was ridiculously easy to get into a judge's robes.

To accomplish that symbolic act, I went to a uniform shop in downtown Detroit that's not far from police headquarters. When I approached the clerk behind the counter and told him I wanted a robe, he never asked me for any identification.

"You looking for a preacher's robe?" the clerk asked.

"No, I'm looking for a judge's robe."

A look of surprise flashed across the elderly gentleman's face before he went and fetched me a large black judge's robe to try on.

When I looked at myself in the mirror and saw myself wearing a judge's robe, I admit that I was a little taken aback. It was definitely a shock to see myself like that. I couldn't help the big grin that started easing across my face.

"Yeah, I'm gonna be the man," I told the dignified jurist smiling back at me in the mirror.

After the clerk looked on in silence for several minutes, his curiosity finally got the better of him. "Where you gonna be a judge at, man?"

"Thirty-sixth District Court," I said, making sure my robe wasn't a high-water version. Nor did I want it to drag the floor.

"What's your name?"

"Mathis."

"Oh, I've heard of you."

I paid $150 in cash for my robe, which I placed in a black hanging bag before I drove away. As had been the case the night before I was elected to the bench, I couldn't get to sleep right away.

We've done it, Mom, was all I could think. We've done it. I made it a point to thank her again for instilling the values of spirituality and education in me, and I promised not to let her down.

The following morning, at ten A.M. on January 5, 1995, the chief judge of the 36th District Court officially swore me in during a private ceremony in a nearly empty courtroom. A ceremonial public swearing-in to which I invited five hundred of my supporters and friends was held later in the day.

On the first day I was supposed to hear cases, I had my clerk postpone all of them. Instead, I sat in on several judges' courtrooms, observing their various styles. Some were stern, some were comical, some came across as indifferent. I figured my best bet was just to be myself.

The following day, prior to running my own courtroom for the first time, I tried to make sure that I had a serious look on my face before approaching the bench. But I was so excited that when I heard the words, "All rise, Thirty-sixth District Court is now in session, Judge Greg Mathis presiding," the biggest grin imaginable spread across my face.

As I stepped up to the bench, I looked down on a holding area filled with desperate-looking prisoners hoping they would be released from the Wayne County Jail on a personal bond. The second they saw my grin, they all started grinning, too, and waving.

My smile disappeared immediately.

I began arraigning the various prostitutes, drunk drivers, and a couple of violent criminals. I arraigned approximately thirty people that morning. It was about an hour and a half worth of arraignments that averaged about three minutes apiece.

That afternoon I heard a couple of landlord/tenant cases. By three o'clock I was finished with my docket for the day. The novelty hadn't worn off, because my adrenaline was running pretty high. For the first time I felt I had a direct impact on the dozens of lives that came before me that day. For several people who had come before me I had conditioned their bond on getting drug treatment. I had required teenagers being tried as young adults remain in school or obtain a GED as a condition of their bail. So I had done some things that I thought would have a positive impact on the lives of the people who had come before me. It was empowering.

The rest of the week was more of the same. I was convinced by the end of the week that I could really make a difference in these people's lives.

Of the thirty-one judges in my district, I was consistently rated among the top five during my first year. In fact, during my nearly five-year tenure on the court, I have remained within the top five.

And I received wide praise from attorneys and others who went before me, even those who were skeptical because of my lack of experience in terms of working as a lawyer. My knowledge of the law and my ability to fairly and efficiently adjudicate cases allayed their misgivings.

I had been approached by a number of people from the entertainment industry who felt that my life story might be worthy of a film. One of them was Detroit playwright Ron Milner, who in the 1980s had written and directed a Broadway play titled *Don't Get God Started*, with the Grammy Award–winning Winans gospel group. In 1991 he wrote and directed the Broadway play *Checkmate*, which starred Denzel Washington, Ruby Dee, and Ossie Davis. Ron and I collaborated in creating a film script about my life that he finished in 1997 and circulated among Hollywood producers and agents. The script generated a fair amount of interest, but no action.

Ron's reaction was to suggest that we do an inspirational stage play based on my life. I was thrilled to know that he thought my life was worthy of his work as a playwright and said I would do whatever he needed to make the play happen.

Our goal was to have a Detroit run, then go national if interest warranted. We tried to find a producer to put up the $150,000 necessary for a Detroit run but were unsuccessful.

So ultimately I went out and raised the $150,000 myself. I took out a second mortgage on my house for $60,000, exhausted all my savings, which came to $25,000, and raised and borrowed the rest. Part of it came from Don Barden, who happens to be from Detroit and is the only African American casino owner in the country. He put up $20,000 in sponsorship money, as did two Greek business and political associates of mine, Ted Gatzaros and his partner, Jim Pappas, who put up $20,000 apiece.

Over the course of several weeks, I wrote down several potential titles that might be seen as inspirational. After giving it a good deal of thought, the title I decided on was *Inner City Miracle,* because I felt that was the one that best represented my life and what I had gone through. Produced by Theresa Ellis, the play opened in Detroit on November 17, 1997, and was an overwhelming success.

Two months later, Ron and I were seeking the financial backing to do a national run of *Inner City Miracle.* I was in my chambers one day when my secretary said that Alonzo Brown, who was then a vice president for television at Motown, was on the phone.

I knew Alonzo through Forrest Hamilton, one of many television and movie producers I had been discussing my life-story project with.

"Write this date down," Alonzo blurted excitedly.

"What date?" I responded, shuffling through some paper on my desk.

"Write today's date down," Alonzo insisted. "It's going to change your life forever."

I stopped what I was doing upon hearing that. "Come on with the bullshit, man," I kidded Alonzo. "Every month you Hollywood guys have some new hype."

"No, no, I'm serious," Alonzo said. "I had a meeting with some brothers whose company has a deal with Warner Brothers. Their company, Blackpearl Productions, has a deal to produce new shows."

Alonzo went on to say that judge shows were hot and Warner Bros. might have an interest in doing a judge show featuring me. I instantly realized that television would allow me to inspire and motivate far more people than I ever could reach in the 36th District Court.

Although highly skeptical, I agreed to fly out to Los Angeles to meet with these Blackpearl brothers and with Warner. Which is how my syndicated Judge Mathis program came to be.

I resigned from the bench in January 1999 to begin taping my program in Chicago, which is a short plane ride from my Detroit-area home.

Within a short time after going on the air, I was thrilled to begin receiving hundreds of letters from parents dealing with troubled youths themselves, as well as from inmates who wrote that my achievements had convinced them to use their time wisely while incarcerated.

Soon after the television show aired, there was a bidding war among national promoters interested in *Inner City Miracle*. I agreed to tour with Al Walsh and Clarence Jones, two longtime African American promoters. I actually appeared in the play, and in a pleasant twist appeared onstage with a childhood friend, gospel recording artist Fred Hammond. Fred and I attended Seventh-Day Adventist church school together in the Detroit area.

After having its name changed to *Been There, Done That*, the play toured twenty-nine cities in 2000 and 2001, helping to spread my inspirational message to the playgoing crowd.

That I have lived a blessed life is beyond dispute. But God willing, I still have several more chapters to write in my life story.

Lest anyone think that I've been co-opted by the bright lights of Hollywood, when my television show reaches the end of its run, I'm going to fulfill the pledge I made as a student at Eastern Michigan University. I will return to public service in some fashion, either in the area of civil rights or as an elected official.